A STUDENT'S GUIDE TO SUCCESS

by
Diane Rossiter and Richard Worth

Las Cruces, New Mexico, U.S.A.

Produced by New England Publishing Associates, Inc. for SOFSOURCE, Inc.

Copy Editing: Barbara Jean DiMauro

Editorial Administration: Ron Formica and Chris Ceplenski

Indexing: Marlene London

Design: Teri Prestash

Page Composition: Teri Prestash

Proofreading: L.E. Hand

Cover Design: David Brackenbury

Library of Congress Catalog Card Number: 98-85250

ISBN 1-57163-904-7

TABLE OF CONTENTS

INTRODUCTION

You can achieve success in school. This book explains how to do it. *A Student's Guide to Success* provides a tool kit—a set of skills you can apply in almost any situation you're likely to encounter during your academic career. As you practice and master these skills, you can achieve higher grades and greater satisfaction from the learning process.

Each chapter presents a specific skill, such as critical thinking or writing, public speaking, or test taking. A **Super Tactic** enables you to apply the skill immediately in an academic area, such as language arts or science, or in an extracurricular activity or an after-school job. Each chapter also contains a **Super Strategy**, which gives you tips on some key aspect of the specific skill—for example, how to write a dynamite opening paragraph in your next composition or how to use eye contact with your audience to improve your impact as a public speaker. You'll also see boxes in each chapter that spotlight an interesting fact or a quote from a well-known person explaining why a skill such as critical thinking is important. **Thumbs Up/Thumbs Down** is another special feature describing some of the dos and don'ts for achieving academic success. Finally, each chapter ends with **For Review,** a self-quiz you can take to ensure that you understand the material, followed by an **At-A-Glance Reference Section,** with reference facts you can use in your courses.

A Student's Guide to Success is designed as a handy, easy-to-use reference. Keep this book on your desk at school or at home. Use it whenever you have a question about how to apply one of the skills discussed in this book. Suppose you want to know the best way to prepare for an essay test; Chapter Six will explain it. Or perhaps you'd like an effective strategy for taking notes in history class; turn to Chapter Three. We've presented all the information in clear, concise, bite-sized pieces so you can digest them quickly and easily.

Spend a little time with this book, and you'll become a better student. Master these skills, and you'll learn the secrets of achieving academic success.

1

WHY YOU NEED STUDY SKILLS

The skills you're going to read about in the next ten chapters presented in this book may be among the most important things you learn while you're in school. Ten years from now, you may not remember all the details of the American Revolution, the causes of volcanic eruptions, or how to solve algebraic equations. But study skills will remain with you because you will use them over and over again. They enable you to think clearly, to master new information you read or receive in class, to communicate that information clearly in speaking, writing, and answering test questions, and finally, to manage your time so you can accomplish more and do it better. These skills are applicable not only in the classroom but also on a job, in your family, and in community activities. School is a preparation for life, and at the heart of that preparation are the skills presented here.

IN THIS CHAPTER, YOU'LL LEARN

- **about the importance of critical thinking skills**
- **why you should try to get more out of class time, writing, and reading assignments**
- **about the positive role that tests play in your academic career**
- **how listening and public speaking skills can help you be more successful**
- **why you should learn to use the library**
- **how time management can help you organize the other skills effectively**

CRITICAL THINKING

This book begins with critical thinking because critical thinking acts as a master switch that opens all the other skills. We apply critical thinking to reading and listening, to writing, public speaking, and answering test questions. Critical thinking is the process of identifying problems, gathering appropriate information, and using that information to solve those problems.

More than a century ago, Alexander Graham Bell used critical thinking to figure out how people in different towns and countries could talk to one another without ever leaving home—the result was his invention, the telephone. More recently, modern innovators have used critical thinking to give people greater access to more information than ever before through the Internet.

You can use critical thinking to solve problems in math and science, in language arts, and in social studies. Frequently, your teacher will present a problem in the form of a question: In William Shakespeare's play, why did Othello kill his wife Desdemona? You're required to provide an answer based solely on

Alexander Graham Bell's critical thinking more than a century ago resulted in the invention of the telephone.

information from the text of the play. Perhaps your teacher wants you to present your answer in a composition or on a test or in an oral report to the class. All these tasks involve critical thinking.

Critical thinking enables you to imagine what isn't there and figure out how to create it. The Egyptians used critical thinking skills to build the pyramids, and modern architects use these same skills to build giant skyscrapers. You can write poetry, develop research papers, and organize talks to deliver at school assemblies—all based on your ability to envision something out of nothing. This book, for example, didn't exist until the authors wrote it. Writing involves taking data and putting it together in a new way. That requires critical thinking.

Critical thinking enables you to question what you're told and wonder if it's true. The Italian astronomer Galileo used critical thinking to question whether Earth was the center of the solar system—a belief that was centuries old. He looked through his telescope, made a number of calculations, and figured out that all planets revolved around the sun, not Earth. You use critical thinking in much the same way. You can question what you read or what you see on television, gather more information if you need it, and decide for yourself what's true and what isn't. That's critical thinking!

"Really, now you ask me," said Alice, very much confused, "I don't think—
"Then you shouldn't talk," said the Hatter.

—Louis Carroll,
Alice's Adventures in Wonderland

GETTING THE MOST OUT OF CLASS

Thinking is based on facts, observations, and opinions. In school, you receive most of this information during classes. Classes are where the academic learning process begins. Classes provide structure to the school day; they also provide structure to learning.

How do you use your time in class? For some students, it's an opportunity to daydream. Perhaps their mind drifts back to the party they attended during the past weekend, or perhaps they leap ahead to the baseball game they're going to watch later in the afternoon or the trip they're going to take during the upcoming school vacation. The present slips away as these students are lost in the past or living in the future. But the present is critically important because the teacher uses class time to communicate valuable information. The classroom provides a learning environment unlike any other:

- *The information may be available nowhere else.* The teacher brings in information from his or her readings and experiences that may not be contained in the textbook. This material may show up on an examination.
- *There's no substitute for a person.* Books are only one source of information. No matter how good your math book may be, for example, it can leave you with unanswered questions. You can't talk to a book. But you can talk to your teacher. Your teacher may give you the best explanation you'll ever receive for how to solve a tough problem.
- *You can take advantage of other students' knowledge*. Remember, classrooms are a group experience. Perhaps you don't understand something but another student does. By listening to what that student says, an issue that was unclear in your own mind may be clarified.
- *You can save yourself time later.* Frequently the teacher reviews

important ideas that are contained in your book. If you pay attention in class, it can cut down the time you need to spend on reading assignments.

- *Attitude is important.* If you sit in class expecting to be bored, you probably won't be disappointed. However, if you see classroom time as an opportunity to enhance your knowledge, it will usually work out that way. Some students are shy—they're afraid to speak up or ask questions; they're afraid of looking foolish in front of their classmates. Remember, if your fellow students knew all the answers, they'd be teaching the course, not sitting in the audience. Don't hesitate to speak and ask questions—that's why you're in class.
- *Class can give you a chance to shine and show off what you know.* It's not like television, where someone in the front of the room does all the entertaining and you sit there like a couch potato. Get involved—participate! Teachers often give you points for participating, and it can have a direct impact on your final grade. Participating is an important way to apply information as you learn new things that will help you remember key facts and concepts.

WRITING WITH A PURPOSE

If you want to know whether you really understand something clearly, try writing about it. That's a major reason writing in school is so important. Suppose you've been asked to write a paper on the high rate of divorce in the United States, which you studied in class. The material seemed straightforward enough when your teacher discussed it. She talked about various theories on why the divorce rate had gone up. These included the state laws that have made divorce easier to obtain, the attitude of many couples today that if their marriage isn't happy they should be able to dissolve it, and the feminist movement, which brought many women into the workplace, making them less dependent on their husbands' income and less willing to remain in unhappy marriages. But your teacher doesn't want you to simply rehash all the information he or she provided. Your teacher asked every student to write an essay in which the student takes a position on the following question: Can the high rate of divorce in the United States be reduced?

This requires you to demonstrate a deep understanding of the class material, organize your ideas logically, and present them clearly on paper. Chapter Four explains in detail how to execute a writing project successfully. Before you get to Chapter Four, there are a few general things to keep in mind when you write:

1. *Remember, clear thinking is the basis of all good writing.* Your readers evaluate the way you think by how well you write. If your thoughts are vague and muddy, these will be reflected in your words and sentences.
2. *Remember, it's "Ready. Aim. Fire!"* Some students start writing before they have any idea about what they want to say. In other words, they fire words onto the page before taking aim at hitting a specific target—presenting and supporting a main point in their writing.
3. *Spend enough time in prewriting.* This is where you organize your ideas, gather your facts, make your outlines—all the things that have to happen before you can begin to write logical prose. Many people tend to rush this part of writing. Don't. Sometimes it takes longer than the actual writing itself.
4. *Enjoy the process.* Students often approach a writing project with only one thing in mind: Getting it over with as soon as possible. Writing is a process of putting words together in a

Take time to organize your thoughts and gather your facts.

way that sounds good to you and to your readers. Sometimes it takes trial and error. You'll try a sentence one way, read it to yourself, then go back and write it again before it sounds just right. Try to keep your mind off simply getting the assignment done. Instead, enjoy the satisfaction of working with language to communicate your ideas.

5. *Find a quiet place to work.* Writing is usually a solitary task, involving one person sitting in front of a blank piece of paper or a computer screen. This may be especially difficult if you're someone who doesn't like being alone. Writing also takes concentration. Most of us can't think clearly with the television on, while our friends are talking to us, or when we're constantly being interrupted by telephone calls. You'll need a quiet place to write where you can focus on the project for a significant block of time without distractions.
6. *Remember, creativity requires hard work.* Sometimes creative ideas come to us in a blinding flash. But frequently they have been preceded by a lot of thought. Clear writing isn't easy because it depends on clear thinking, which takes hard work.

It was the inventor Thomas Edison who said: "Genius is one percent inspiration and ninety-nine percent perspiration." Keep that in mind when you sit down to begin your next writing project.

PUTTING ALL THE SKILLS TOGETHER

This chart explains how all the skills presented in this book fit together. Beside each skill is the chapter in which it is fully explained.

SKILLS IN THIS BOOK	EXPLAINED IN CHAPTER:
Communication	4, 6, 9
Critical Thinking	2
Effective Reading	5
Getting the Most Out of Class	3
Information Gathering	3, 5, 7, 8
Information Management	8
Listening	7
Organizing	2, 10
Public Speaking	9
Test Taking	6
Time Management	10
Writing with a Purpose	4

EFFECTIVE READING

Most of the time you spend studying and doing homework involves reading. This isn't the same as reading for pleasure. When you read a mystery story, for example, you're usually content to be carried along by the plot until you get to the end and find out "whodunit". In school, you read with a specific purpose in mind. As you can see from the chart in the Super Strategy feature, reading is one of the information-gathering skills covered in this book. As you go along in your reading assignment, you're expected to pick up information, then use it in communication—writing papers, delivering oral presentations, and taking examinations.

There's a lot of reading to do in junior high school and high school and a great deal of information to absorb. In fact, there probably aren't enough hours in the day to learn it. You constantly have to make decisions about what is important and what isn't—what you should remember and what you can just as easily forget. One of the primary goals of this book is to teach you how to work smart and how to use your time as efficiently as possible. To work smart, you have to learn how to read smart.

- *Do your reading assignments when you're fresh.* You can't read a textbook the way you read an adventure novel. So don't put off your important reading homework until late at night when you're likely to feel exhausted and want to go to sleep. If you do, you won't get very much out of the reading and will probably have to do it over again.
- *Look for visual cues.* Most textbooks use a highly visual layout. That's true of this book too. A great deal of important information is set off in headlines or highlighted for you through the use of bullets, boldface, and italics. These devices break up the text and make the page more interesting. That doesn't mean you shouldn't read the information in the text. It contains key details that you should know. But many of the important ideas have already been marked for you by the author and publisher of the book. Follow these cues, take note of the key ideas, and you can save yourself a lot of time.

- *Pace yourself.* Many students find it difficult to read in one subject area for much more than an hour. Any longer, and they begin to lose focus. Don't overdo it. Read for a while, then take a break. Or switch to another task, such as doing math problems. By pacing yourself, you'll retain far more information.
- *Read and relate. Don't read in a vacuum.* Try to relate what you're reading to what you heard in the classroom, read in a newspaper or magazine, or saw on television. Make as many connections as you can; that will enhance the reading process.

12 TEST TAKING

Exams! It's a word that sends shivers up the spines of even top students. So much of education seems to revolve around tests. And your scores may spell the difference between success and failure. It doesn't always seem fair, but that's the reality of the school environment.

Is there an easy way to prepare for exams? Some students resort to cheating. You've probably heard of incidents in which a student breaks into a teacher's desk and steals the test questions. Not only is cheating morally wrong, it's also risky, stupid, and unfair. It's risky because those who do it could and should be expelled. It's stupid because it undermines the purpose of testing—to find out what students know and whether they've really mastered the subject. It's unfair because it devalues the accomplishments of everyone else who had to study hard to get their grades.

Most people tend to focus on the negative side of testing and worry about choking during an exam. But there are some positive aspects to test taking. Testing gives you an opportunity to review the material that you've covered in a class. This review reinforces the information and implants it more firmly in your memory. It also gives you a chance to put all the information together to see if it makes sense. This process is called **synthesizing.** It's a valuable skill that you'll use again and again in school and on a job. Many essay questions ask you to synthesize material. For example, a question on your English test may ask: "After reading Macbeth and Othello by William Shakespeare, what conclusions can you draw about the key elements of a Shakespearean hero?"

Some tests are comprised of multiple choice or short-answer questions that emphasize the recall of details. Many students don't like this type of exam because it relies too much on memory. But you should never underestimate the importance of having all the important details at your fingertips. Your success in school and in many types of jobs will greatly depend on knowing the facts and figures, then presenting them effectively to your teachers, your boss, your coworkers and your customers.

MEMORY TRICK: L R R

Tests don't occur every day. But your preparation for them should go on almost daily. It will make the process of actually taking an exam much simpler.

LISTEN. Pay attention to what your teacher emphasizes. It is likely to appear on a test.

READ. Do all your reading assignments. They'll also be the source of test questions.

REVIEW. Regular reviews will keep you prepared for surprise quizzes and cut down your study time for exams.

"It is the disease of not listening...that I am troubled withal."

—William Shakespeare

LISTENING

Most people have been in a situation in which someone was talking to them but they didn't hear what the person said because they were thinking about something else. Listening involves more than sounds going into one's ears. It also requires using the critical thinking skills mentioned earlier. You have to evaluate what you hear and put it together with other information so you can use it effectively.

You spend so much time listening that you're probably not aware of how valuable a skill it is—until you make a mistake because you failed to listen carefully. Perhaps this has happened at home when you weren't listening to something your parents said. Or maybe you have an after-school job and made a mistake because you weren't paying attention when your boss explained the directions for carrying out a new procedure.

Listening in class is particularly important. As we explained in an earlier section, listening is how you acquire much of the information you'll need to succeed in school. Once the material is presented, the teacher assumes that you understand it—that is, unless you raise your hand and ask a question. But if you weren't listening, how will you know whether you understood the material or not? As a result, you may have missed an opportunity to have a difficult concept clearly explained to you by your teacher. You have a choice: use class time efficiently or waste it. Working smart in class means listening smart.

- *Participate in the discussion.* Listening is not a passive activity, the way watching television is. Listening requires active involvement. Ask yourself: Do I understand what's being covered? How does it connect to what I've read in my textbook? Do I need to ask a question?

- *Concentrate on what is said—and how it is said.* In Chapter Seven, you'll learn that a speaker uses more than words to make important points. A speaker relies on nonverbal language—gestures, facial expressions, and tone of voice. You have to focus on all these things to get the complete message. This applies to classroom lectures as well as to conversations. Perhaps you've had the experience of presenting a new idea to someone, and the one word response was: "Great!" Depending on the person's facial expression and tone of voice, "great" can mean "terrific" or "awful." You have to see and hear the nonword cues.
- *Focus on what's important. Not everything you hear will be important.* Your job as a listener is to separate the wheat from the chaff. Listen for the main ideas and write them in your class notes. If it's directions for carrying out a homework assignment, make sure you understand all the key steps.
- *Digest what you've heard:* Listening is a way of gathering information. But you can't really possess the material and make it your own until you use it. This registers what you've learned in your memory and ensures that you completely understand it. Suppose you've just covered a difficult concept in second period math class. Try to use it as soon after the class as possible. In your fourth period study hall, for example, do your math homework. Then, if there's anything you don't quite understand, you can find the teacher and ask some additional questions.

INFORMATION MANAGEMENT

Like listening, information management is another skill that you use to gather data. One of the richest sources of data available to us is the library. The first libraries were created 4,000 years ago and consisted of a few stone tablets. Imagine trying to take those home with you! Today, the information in libraries is much easier to use and far more extensive. This can be good and bad. There are more resources for you to use in your research. But accessing all this material can seem like a formidable task, especially if you don't know your way around a library very well. There are book stacks and magazine collections, videotapes and audio recordings, as well as information stored in all kinds of computer databases and on the Internet.

There's nothing that can seem more frustrating than wandering around a library looking for something without having a clue where to find it. Three strategies will help you get more out of the library.

First, if you don't know, ask. The librarians are there to help you. They're accustomed to answering questions from patrons. Don't forget that one of the main functions of any library is to serve people like you who are looking for information.

Second, once you've asked your question, listen carefully as the librarian explains how to find the data you need. Perhaps the explanation will be easy. You can just use the computer to locate one or two books in the library's collection. But perhaps your project is more complicated, involving several of the library's databases. Make sure the librarian shows you how to use them. Then, try accessing the information yourself before the librarian leaves to help someone else. That way, if you're having a problem, you can ask a question.

Third, be patient. Finding what you want may take time. You're like a detective engaged in solving a mystery. Enjoy the process of

One of the richest sources of data available to us is the library.

looking for information rather than simply being focused on getting the job done so you can leave the library as soon as possible. Remember, you're learning a skill that will be essential throughout your education and just as valuable later when you go to work.

PUBLIC SPEAKING

One of the most important skills in organizations today is public speaking. If you're someone who can stand in front of a group or at a meeting and convince an audience of your point of view, you'll have the word *leader* written all over you. It's easy to assume that effective speaking is a natural talent. You have it or you don't. But that's not true. You can learn to be a good speaker. However, it takes work. And for most people that work has to begin early—while they're still in school.

- *Grab the opportunities.* Many people shy away from public speaking because they're afraid to do it. But you won't become any better if you don't practice. Sure, you'll probably make some mistakes at first. Everybody does. But you'll improve.

One of the most important skills in organizations today is public speaking.

And the more public speaking you do, the less anxiety you'll have about doing it.

- *Remember the audience.* As you'll discover in Chapter Nine, good speakers focus on their listeners. They know that if the audience tunes out, there's no reason to continue speaking. These speakers try to present information in a way that will interest the listeners. And they know how to put enthusiasm into their delivery so the audience will stay tuned in.
- *Don't overdo it.* Most listeners become restless after a short period of time. Keep your talk short and don't try to cover too much. Present one main idea and the details you need to support it. That's enough for any talk.
- *Don't wait until the last minute.* Leave yourself plenty of time to prepare the presentation. If you're delivering an oral report in class, you may need to gather information from your textbook, your class notes, and the library. You'll also need time to practice your delivery to make it just as powerful as you can.

Leaders in organizations spend about 1/3 of their day speaking.

TIME MANAGEMENT

Time management provides the organizing principles that enable you to use all the skills presented in this book most efficiently. If you're one of those people who feels tired at the end of the day, and goes to bed without completing an important task, then better time management is a skill you really need. To work smart, you have to plan smart.

- *Time management requires planning.* If you're not someone who's used to planning, now's the time to start.
- *Time management requires setting priorities.* Some people seem content to let events rule their lives. They're easily distracted from doing important things by whatever comes up in the course of the day. If their friends ask them to go to the mall, for example, they forget about the book report they're supposed to write, and it doesn't get done on time. If you want to be successful in school, you have to get your priorities straight and stick with them.
- *Time management requires critical thinking.* You constantly have to ask yourself: How can I use my time best? If you're going to have a discussion in English class on Romeo and Juliet, then the study hall just before English may be the best time to review your notes. This helps you get the most out of your class.
- *Time management involves taking the long view.* Many projects have a long timeline. A social studies paper, for example, may be due in two months. But you can make efficient use of your

other skills—reading, information management, listening, and writing— only if you give yourself enough time to do the project well. That means getting started early and planning the project carefully.

SCHOOLED FOR SUCCESS

THUMBS UP
Successful Students

Use critical thinking to provide greater insight into what they hear, read, and see.

Use the classroom as a learning laboratory to enhance their understanding of information.

Decide what they want to say before beginning to write, then try to enjoy the writing process.

Read Smart—looking for visual cues to what's important and relate them to other materials.

Focus on the positive aspects of tests as a means of synthesizing information and mastering details.

Learn how to take advantage of the library as a valuable resource.

Seize opportunities to make speeches to help improve their public speaking skills.

Plan smart—utilize the skills of time management.

THUMBS DOWN
Unsuccessful Students

Fire words on the page as fast as possible so they can get the writing assignment over quickly.

Read with no specific purpose except to get their homework done.

Look for the easy way around tests and sometimes resort to cheating.

Avoid the library at all costs because the quantity of material there is overwhelming.

Let the fear of public speaking prevent them from doing it.

Avoid planning, scheduling, and setting priorities.

SUPER TACTICS

MASTERING HIGH SCHOOL

As each year goes by, you'll find your workload in school increasing. You'll be asked to juggle more and more projects. That's why there's no time like the present to begin mastering the skills presented in this book. Indeed, by the time you reach your senior year, these skills will be critical to getting everything done on time and completing it to the best of your ability. As a senior, you may find yourself not only with classes to attend and homework assignments to complete but also with participating in a varsity sport, editing the yearbook, holding down an after-school job, participating in a community volunteer activity, or taking college admission tests and filling out applications.

Here are some tactics you can apply to every subject you take that will enable you to integrate the nine skills presented in this book, use them to your maximum advantage, and make high school a much more enjoyable experience.

- Avoid needless duplication. It's easy to waste a lot of time because you're not prepared. For example, if you haven't done the reading assignment to prepare for class, that class will be far less valuable to you. Instead of really understanding what the teacher is talking about, a great deal of it may go over your head. Then you'll have to go back over the reading assignment again or talk to the teacher to get clarification on what was discussed in class. In short, you'll have gone through a lot of needless duplication of effort. It's much easier to be prepared. Then you'll get more out of class, out of your reading, and out of listening to the teacher.
- Get it right the first time. Some students rush through their read-

ing assignments and get very little out of them. They do the same with writing projects—hurry through the first draft just so it's done. Unfortunately, too much remains undone. They don't really understand what they've read and have to reread the homework, perhaps several times. And their report still needs an enormous amount of work because it wasn't written correctly. Make your first pass at something as close to your best as you can. Oh, yes, you'll still have to go back to that paper and make a few changes. But by doing things right the first time, you'll save a great deal of time later. There's no bigger time-waster than undoing what you've already done and doing the same job all over again.

- Don't let little problems become big ones. If there was something you didn't understand in class or in your reading assignment, don't let it go. By not fully comprehending an important concept, a little problem can grow into a much bigger one. Understanding that concept may hold the key to understanding others. As a result, future reading assignments may not be as meaningful to you. And your score on the next test may be lower than you'd like. Deal with the problem when it occurs, don't put it off until later.
- Be persistent. If you can't solve a difficult problem in one of your classes, don't give up. Look for information in your textbook. Talk to people—your teacher, other students or your parents. If necessary, go to the library and make use of its resources. Persistence is one of the most valuable traits you can develop in school. It will help you penetrate the surface of what you read, make you smarter in class, raise your test scores, and improve your writing projects and oral reports. In short, persistence applied to the nine skills presented in this book will make you a more successful student.

FOR REVIEW

1. How can you use critical thinking in school?
2. Why is class time so valuable?
3. Why is prewriting important before you sit down to write a paper?
4. What is smart reading?
5. What are the positive aspects of test taking?
6. What are four elements of smart listening?
7. How can you make the most of the information found in a library?
8. Why should you grab every opportunity to practice public speaking?
9. How can time management help you work smarter?

2 CRITICAL THINKING—YOUR KEY TO SUCCESS

Critical thinking. Perhaps you've begun to see and hear these words in some of your textbooks and from many of your teachers. *Uh oh,* you think, *something new to learn.*

Relax. Critical thinking doesn't require you to stuff more information into your already overtaxed brain. But it does require that you apply your brain power in some challenging ways. And it's not really new—you use critical thinking whenever you analyze information and use that information to solve problems or draw conclusions. Critical thinking is the kind of thinking that will help you make decisions and take actions that lead to academic achievement and personal success.

The first challenge in critical thinking is to accurately interpret what you hear and read—and even what you feel. This chapter will help sharpen the skills you to need to do this.

IN THIS CHAPTER YOU WILL LEARN WAYS TO CAREFULLY :

- **clarify**
- **analyze**
- **infer**
- **predict**
- **evaluate**

HOW IMPORTANT IS CRITICAL THINKING?

Critical thinking is an approach to learning that is so important that successful completion of a critical-thinking course is a requirement for graduation for the entire 19-campus California State University system. Critical thinking skills are used in all levels of education and in all subject areas. You will need to think critically in order to:

- take a stand on an issue and defend your position
- evaluate the historical significance of an event
- solve word problems in mathematics
- predict the consequences of a specific political action
- write a persuasive essay
- formulate and test a hypothesis for a lab report
- compare the characters of the protagonists in two short stories

"Learning without thought is a labor lost; thought without learning is perilous"

—Confucius

CRITICAL THINKING AND TEST PERFORMANCE

Tests today demand that students do more than simply recall facts. You are asked to interpret, discuss, and explain. On essay tests, you are expected to give responses that are focused, well-organized, and supported with significant details. Even standardized multiple-choice tests sometimes call on students to analyze information and infer meanings from passages. Only students experienced in critical thinking perform well on these kinds of tests.

CRITICAL THINKING AND PROBLEM SOLVING

In critical thinking, the emphasis is on using logical reasoning to analyze information and draw conclusions from that information. This is how problems are solved in school and in the real world. There are four basic components to critical thinking:

MEMORY TRICK:

P I S E

P Identifying the **Problem**
I Gathering appropriate **Information**
S Using this information to **Solve** the problem
E **Evaluating** the solution or conclusion

The sections that follow will help you understand the process of critical thinking and apply it to what you read and write.

IDENTIFYING THE PROBLEM

You cannot begin to solve a problem until you have identified and clarified that problem. For example, in history class you are asked to interpret this quote by Abraham Lincoln:

> *"A house divided against itself cannot stand. I believe this government cannot endure, permanently half* slave *and half* free."

To identify the problem, express it as a question: Why did Lincoln believe the United States could not endure if it were half slave and half free? To further clarify the problem, identify the central issues: Lincoln considered slavery a moral issue, but he also realized it was a political and an economic issue as well. Clarifying the issues of a problem will steer you in the right direction as you begin to gather information.

With the ability to access information by the stroke of a computer key comes the responsibility of verifying the accuracy and validity of that information.

GATHERING APPROPRIATE INFORMATION

Gathering information is at the core of making a decision, solving a problem, or reaching a conclusion. For information to be appropriate, it must be relevant to the problem: It must *relate* to the central issues of the problem. It is also essential that the information be valid. The critical thinker judges the *quality* of the information he or she gathers. He or she weighs the information for consistency and checks it for bias.

Compare several sources; never rely on just one. Be particularly skeptical of information on the Internet. A web site may have been designed by someone with very little knowledge of the subject or even someone with an ax to grind. With the ability to access information by the stroke of a computer key comes the responsibility of verifying the accuracy and validity of that information.

Printed material—books, magazines, newspapers—also needs to be evaluated. Video may grab our attention, but its emotional impact must be taken into account. Whatever the source of information, it is your job to give it only the weight it deserves.

THE QUALITY OF INFORMATION

To judge the quality of information, first determine if it is fact or opinion. If it is opinion, carefully consider the source of the information. Here are some important questions to ask:

- Is the source by an authority or expert in the field?
- Is the opinion reached by careful reasoning and presented as the conclusion of a detailed, well-supported argument?
- Is the argument presented in a logical order?
- Is it based (in whole or in part) on any mistaken assumptions?
- Are there any unsupported generalizations?
- Are all statements in the source consistent?

Even if the conclusion was reached through logical, reasoned judgment, the source needs to be examined for bias.

- Does the author of the source have a conflict of interest? (Would the author benefit by a particular position being accepted?)
- Does the argument appeal to emotion rather than to logic?
- Are there any stereotypes presented in the information? (These may not be valid and often signal bias.)
- Is the information slanted to fit a particular value or prejudice?

PERSONAL BIAS, MISCONCEPTIONS, AND ASSUMPTIONS

In addition to judging the source's possible bias, you must take care to guard against any personal bias. Your values and prejudices may lead you to a slanted interpretation of the information. Seek out sources of information that present differing points of view, not just sources that mirror your view.

Problems in evaluating information can also arise from misconceptions and assumptions. Below is an example of how all three—bias, misconception, and assumption—lead to a misinterpretation of perfectly correct information.

Let's suppose that for your term project in U.S. History you choose to research the effects of labor unions on female factory workers in the 1890s. You don't know much about 19th-century labor unions, but you come from a long family line of union members. You expect to determine that the unions protected the female workers' rights and improved their standard of living. *(Your **bias** in favor of unions may lead you to view unions in a totally positive light.)*

Your research produces information about the founding of the American Federation of Labor (AFL) in 1886. Led by Samuel Gompers, this national union fought to secure better wages, hours, and conditions for its workers. You find statistics that show the *median* wage of unionized factory workers rose steadily in the 1890s. In your report you write that *average* wages increased. *(Your teacher later points out that many people share your **misconception** that median and average are the same.)*

You conclude that unions had a positive effect on female factory workers. *(You **assumed** the AFL and other unions welcomed female members in 1890. The AFL and many other unions **did not**.)*

As you can see, bias in favor of something can cause misinterpretation as readily as prejudice against something can. To think critically, it is essential to guard against bias, misconceptions, and assumptions in yourself as well as in the information you examine. Judgment must be based on reason and supported by evidence, not emotion.

USING THE INFORMATION TO SOLVE THE PROBLEM

Once you have gathered sufficient appropriate information, you can begin to connect that information to solve the problem or reach a conclusion. Analyze the information carefully to discover relationships among the pieces of information. The relationships will not always be obvious; however, if discovered and understood, they will point to a solution or conclusion. Facts alone do not solve problems—but the meanings you infer from the facts may.

"Elementary, my Dear Watson"

Sherlock: ***Then, having established ourselves upon this sound basis (of facts), it is our duty to see what inferences may be drawn.***

Watson: ***Though most of the facts were familiar to me, I had not sufficiently appreciated their relative importance, nor their connection to each other.***

—from the short story "Silver Blaze" by Arthur Conan Doyle

Sherlock Holmes, the most famous fictional detective, had legendary powers of deduction. Deductions are inferences made after seeing how facts relate to one another. Holmes was a master at perceiving subtle relationships among the facts and connecting them in a logical way to solve his cases. He did not feel this was a remarkable talent. To him, this was simply "elementary."

It may not seem so simple to you, but you already use some of the skills required. You formulate questions, make comparisons, consider the context, and look for cause and effect. These are tools that can help you connect information in a way that will lead to a solution or conclusion. You will find some specific suggestions in the Super Strategy section of this chapter.

"At Learning's fountain it is sweet to drink
But 'tis a nobler privilege to think."

—J. G. Saxe, poet

AVOIDING MISTAKES IN LOGIC

As you look for ways to connect information, be sure to use sound reasoning. The inferences you make should not be hasty generalizations based on a small bit of "evidence." The evidence should be broad; otherwise, it's possible that it is actually an exception. For example, a medical researcher would never use only three positive-outcome cases to "prove" the effectiveness of a new drug. Likewise, you will need to examine enough evidence to be sure that results you are looking at are typical, not exceptional.

That same researcher would also not hastily conclude cause and effect based on what may just be circumstance: 50 short people ate rice pudding as toddlers; therefore, rice pudding causes short stature. The cause-and-effect links you make must be arrived at rationally. You don't have to be Sherlock Holmes, but you do have to be logical.

Train yourself to reject illogical reasoning in information sources and in your interpretation of that information. Only then will you be in a position to understand, interpret, and evaluate

Examine enough evidence to be sure that results you are looking at are typical, not exceptional.

information in ways that help you solve a problem or reach a conclusion.

Some common mistakes in logic appear in the Thumbs Down feature on this page. Be sure to avoid these pitfalls. The Thumbs Up section reviews a positive approach to solving problems through critical thinking.

CRITICAL THINKING

THUMBS UP if you:

- clarify the thesis, question, or problem
- keep the situation (context) in mind
- judge the credibility of sources carefully
- recognize and reject irrelevant statements
- recognize assumptions; reject them if they're mistaken
- recognize and reject inconsistencies
- recognize and avoid bias

THUMBS DOWN if you:

- are close-minded or biased
- persist in misconceptions when there is evidence to the contrary
- assume that what is true of exceptional cases is also true of typical cases
- infer cause and effect when evidence does not support it
- accept inconsistencies and illogical reasoning in a source
- compare two things that are not appropriately similar
- make hasty generalizations and conclusions

EVALUATING THE SOLUTION OR CONCLUSION

You may be so happy to reach a conclusion that you stop there. Don't! Whether you are drawing a conclusion by analyzing sources of information or presenting your reasoned argument (written or oral), continue to think critically. Test that conclusion very carefully. Ask yourself the following "test" questions:

1. Does the conclusion explain all the facts?
2. Are any facts inconsistent with the conclusion?
3. Are there any other reasonable conclusions?
4. Is every other possible conclusion inconsistent with the facts?

The answers to the first and last questions should be yes, to the other two, no. If you do find inconsistencies, retrace your line of reasoning. You will find some helpful suggestions in the Super Strategy section below.

SUPER STRATEGY

TECHNIQUES IN CRITICAL THINKING

These are strategies that can direct your original line of reasoning; return to them if your conclusion does not satisfy the four test questions.

- **Be a skeptic. Critical thinkers question everything. Ask searching questions, such as Why? Demand that reasons given as evidence be proven, not simply stated as fact. Watch for assumptions and test them for accuracy and truth.**
- **Take a closer look. Carefully examine (and reexamine) reasoning based on comparisons or cause and effect. Is the comparison an**

appropriate one that adds strength to the argument? Is there true cause and effect, or are the elements actually unrelated?

- Question yourself. Ask: Is this making sense? Is this line of reasoning going anywhere? Should I try something different? Question your assumptions: What makes me think that? Could I be wrong?
- Be open-minded. Look for opposing views. Other views can help you generate alternate conclusions. Don't simply reject information that goes against something you believe to be true—your belief could be based on a misconception.
- Look at information in different ways. Rearrange and reposition the information you are considering. Like in a kaleidoscope, a new pattern may emerge. See the pattern and the solution is within your grasp.
- Map it out. Making the problem visual can help to solve it. Make lists, charts, pictures, and diagrams. Make graphic word maps (see the examples on pages 53-54). These will often uncover hidden connections that point to a solution.
- Write it out. Putting your thoughts into words on paper helps make clear what you know and don't know. Realizing what you don't know can sometimes point you in the right direction.
- Talk it out. If possible, talk it out with someone else. Ask others to be skeptical, to pinpoint mistakes in logic. Brainstorm with others for alternate solutions.
- Try it out. There are often multiple ways to solve a problem. Think about strategies you have used successfully in the past to solve similar problems. Apply the known strategy to the new problem—it may work. If you or someone else comes up with another possible solution or conclusion, give it a try: Test it with the four questions at the beginning of this section.

LEARN FROM EVALUATING THE SOLUTION

When you evaluate your solution, do more than check that your conclusion is reasonable and logical. Think about the procedure you used: How did it help you solve the problem? By evaluating the strategies you used to solve your problem, you learn what works.

Perhaps working backward was effective in solving a particular kind of word problem in your math class. Think about why that was a good tactic for that problem. Ask yourself how you reached the conclusion in one case so that you will be able to apply that processes to a new question or problem. As you become more conscious of your thought process, you will begin to discover more ways to solve problems.

CRITICAL THINKING IN SCIENCE

Scientific thinking is critical thinking. You can learn scientific facts and formulas by memorizing them, but you cannot understand scientific concepts without critical thinking. Let's explore how scientific thinking involves the four components of critical thinking.

1. **Identifying the problem. You are studying a unit on water. When you get to the section in your text on freezing, you and most of your classmates begin to feel lost. Your teacher breaks up the class into brainstorming groups. The assignment is to formulate questions that relate to freezing. Your group wants to know why ice occupies more space than an equivalent weight of water. This question will direct your next step.**
2. **Gathering appropriate information. Scientific knowledge changes rapidly. It is essential to use sources of information that**

Understanding scientific facts requires critical thinking skills.

are up to date. Scientists get information from two sources: from books and journals that publish the works of other scientists and from their own observations of the natural world.

If you are having difficulty reading a book or article, use some of the strategies from Chapter Five: Effective Reading. Then evaluate the quality of the information, as suggested previously in this chapter. For example, make sure that the information is appropriate. Information on the freezing of other substances will not necessarily be relevant to the freezing of water.

Often scientific knowledge comes from designing and conducting experiments in a laboratory. If the source material you are using is based on someone's observations, it is especially important to judge how carefully those observations were made and reported.

Scientists follow an established procedure for conducting research and experiments. This is called the *scientific method.*

The steps for this procedure are listed in the Reference section at the end of this chapter. Lab reports are also based on the scientific method. Results of research are published in professional journals. In judging the quality of information and conclusions based on experiments, you need to be sure the researcher used the established procedures of the scientific community.

"Equipped with his five senses, man explores the universe around him and calls the adventure science."

—Edwin Powell Hubble, scientist

Or perhaps the observations will be made by you. Your textbook or your teacher may suggest an experiment that could help answer your question. You carefully gather, record, and organize the data (information) that results from your experiment. Of course, you must also use established procedures in planning and conducting your experiment. Your teacher will tell you the specific lab report format to use, but general guidelines are provided in the Reference section at the end of this chapter.

3. Using the information to solve the problem. To solve a scientific problem, think like a detective. You need to analyze and interpret ideas and information in an orderly way. Like Sherlock Holmes, you need to think deductively: Each idea leads to another. By classifying, measuring, and comparing data, you begin to see how the data are related.

As stated earlier in this chapter, the inferences you draw from your information cannot be made hastily. They should come from a thorough examination of a broad sampling of evidence. Use a variety of strategies (see the Super Strategy section) to help you see how the ideas and information are connected. As you discover these relationships, the conclusion may become clear.

4. Evaluating the solution. Scientific research does not always resolve a question or problem. But scientists know that they can learn a great deal even when their work does not lead to a clear conclusion. A most important objective of critical thinking is to discover weaknesses in the reasoning process.

Perhaps you do not have enough background knowledge to be able to see how the data relates to the problem. You may need to read additional sources or talk to someone more knowledgeable. You may need to go back over the information; especially reexamine any assumed cause and effect. If an experiment is involved, recheck your procedures; a simple mistake there can skew your results.

As a final step, consider any new questions that occur to you. These questions may point you in the right direction. In trying to solve the new problem, you may solve your original one as well.

FOR REVIEW

1. What are the four components of critical thinking?
2. What are some questions to ask when judging the quality of information?
3. What are deductions? What are inferences?
4. What are some skills that help you make logical deductions?
5. What are some common mistakes in logic?
6. How do you make a reasoned argument?
7. What are four questions to ask in testing a conclusion?
8. What can you learn from evaluating a conclusion or a solution to a problem?

SCIENTIFIC METHOD

1. **Identify and state the problem.** What do you want to find out? It may help to formulate a question.

2. **Gather information.** Read about your problem, especially work done by other.

3. **Hypothesize or predict.** Consider what you know already. What do you think will happen? Make a clear statement of what you expect the out come to be.

4. **Design and carry out an experiment.** Plan an experiment to test your hypothesis. What steps will you need to take? Follow the procedure carefully; make precise measurements and calculations.

5. **Make detailed observations and record data.** Observe your experiment and carefully record and organize any data it produces; use drawings, charts, tables, graphs, and diagrams.

6. **Analyze your data.** Look for trends or patterns in the data. Do the results solve the problem? If they don't, think about why they don't. Do you need more information?

7. **State your conclusion.** Conclude whether or not the data support your hypothesis. If not, try to come up with another way to explore your problem.

LAB REPORT FORMAT

All lab reports are based on the scientific method. The brief outline below is just a guideline; your teacher will provide you with an exact format to follow.

1. **Title.** Write a brief title that indicates what the lab report is about.
2. **Purpose.** Explain the objectives of the experiment. Describe the problem or hypothesis and how the experiment was designed to test the hypothesis.
3. **Materials and procedure.** Describe how you conducted the experiment. Be orderly and complete in describing the procedures and equipment.
4. **Results.** Organize and summarize the data your experiment produced. Use tables and graphs to present data; describe important findings in narrative form.
5. **Conclusions.** Discuss the results in regard to your hypothesis. Base your conclusions on your interpretation of the data.

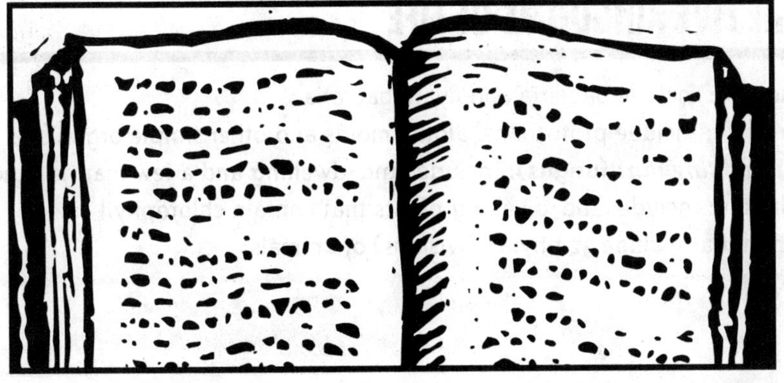

SCIENTIFIC MEASUREMENTS

Scientists express measurements of weight, volume, length, and temperature in metric terms. Below are some tables of metric terms.

Length	Volume	Mass (weight)
km = kilometer (1000m)	kl = kiloliter (1000l)	kg = kilogram, (1000g)
m = meter	**l = liter**	**g = gram**
dm = decimeter (.1m)	dl = deciliter (.1 l)	dg = decigram (.1g)
cm = centimeter (.01m)	cl = centiliter (.01 l)	cg = centigram (.01g)
mm= millimeter (.001m)	ml* = milliliter (.001 l)	mg = milligram (.001g)

* 1 ml also = 1 cc (cubic centimeter) of H_2O

CONVERSION FACTORS:

for Length	1 inch = 2.54 cm	1 cm = 0.394 inch
for Volume	1 quart = 946 ml	1 liter = 1.06 quart
for Mass	1 oz. = 28.35 grams	1 pound (lb) = 454 grams

Temperature: Fahrenheit to Celsius—subtract 32 from Fahrenheit temperature and multiply the result by $5/9$ (0.555); (°F - 32) x $5/9$
Celsius to Fahrenheit—multiply Celsius temperature by $9/5$ (1.8) and add 32 to the result; (°C x $9/5$) + 32

THE FIVE KINGDOMS OF LIFE

Monera: include bacteria and cyanobacteria
Protista: include protozoans, algae, molds and other simple organisms
Fungi (*singular:* fungus): include land-dwelling and a few marine fungi
Plantae: include land-dwelling plants that contain chlorophyll
Animalia: include 32 phyla (divisions) of animals

CLASSIFICATION OF ORGANISMS (TAXONOMY)

Category	**Corn**	**Katydid**	**Human**
Kingdom	Plantae	Animalia	Animalia
Phylum	Anthophyta	Arthropoda	Chordata
Class	Monocotyledones	Insecta	Mammalia
Order	Commelinales	Orthoptera	Primates
Family	Poaceae	Tettigoniidae	Hominidae
Genus	Zea	Scudderia	Homo
Species	*Zea mays*	*Scudderia carolinensis*	*Homo sapiens*

PERIODIC TABLE

1 Group IA	2 IIA	3 IIIA IIIB	4 IVA IVB	5 VA VB	6 VIA VIB	7 VIIA VIIB	8	9 VIIIA VIII	10	11 IB	12 IIB	13 IIIB IIIA	14 IVB IVA	15 VB VA	16 VIB VIA	17 VIIB VIIA	17 VIIIA
1 **H** 1.01																	2 **He** 4.00
3 **Li** 6.94	4 **Be** 9.01											5 **B** 10.81	6 **C** 12.01	7 **N** 14.01	8 **O** 15.99	9 **F** 18.99	10 **Ne** 20.18
11 **Na** 22.99	12 **Mg** 24.30											13 **Al** 26.99	14 **Si** 28.08	15 **P** 30.97	16 **S** 32.06	17 **Cl** 35.45	18 **Ar** 39.94
19 **K** 39.10	20 **Ca** 40.08	21 **Sc** 44.96	22 **Ti** 47.90	23 **V** 50.94	24 **Cr** 51.99	25 **Mn** 54.94	26 **Fe** 55.85	27 **Co** 58.93	28 **Ni** 58.71	29 **Cu** 63.55	30 **Zn** 65.37	31 **Ga** 69.72	32 **Ge** 72.59	33 **As** 74.92	34 **Se** 78.96	35 **Br** 79.90	36 **Kr** 83.80
37 **Rb** 85.47	38 **Sr** 87.62	39 **Y** 88.90	40 **Zr** 91.22	41 **Nb** 92.91	42 **Mo** 95.94	43 **Tc** (98)	44 **Ru** 101.07	45 **Rh** 102.90	46 **Pd** 106.4	47 **Ag** 107.87	48 **Cd** 112.40	49 **In** 114.82	50 **Sn** 118.69	51 **Sb** 121.75	52 **Te** 127.60	53 **I** 126.90	54 **Xe** 131.30
55 **Cs** 132.90	56 **Ba** 137.34	57 **La** 138.91	72 **Hf** 178.49	73 **Ta** 180.95	74 **W** 180.95	75 **Re** 186.2	76 **Os** 190.2	77 **Ir** 192.2	78 **Pt** 195.09	79 **Au** 196.97	80 **Hg** 200.59	81 **Tl** 204.37	82 **Pb** 207.19	83 **Bi** 208.98	84 **Po** 208.98	85 **At** 209.98	86 **Rn** 222.02
87 **Fr** 223.02	88 **Ra** 226.03	89 **Ac** 227.03	104 **Unq** 261.10	105 **Unp** 262.11	106 **Unh** 263.12	107 **Uns** 262.12	108 **Uno**	109 **Une**									

58 **Ce** 140.12	59 **Pr** 140.90	60 **Nd** 144.24	61 **Pm** 146.91	62 **Sm** 150.34	63 **Eu** 151.95	64 **Gd** 157.25	65 **Tb** 158.92	66 **Dy** 162.50	67 **Ho** 164.93	68 **Er** 167.26	69 **Tm** 168.93	70 **Yb** 173.04	71 **Lu** 174.97
90 **Th** 232.04	91 **Pa** 231.04	92 **U** 238.01	93 **Np** 237.05	94 **Pu** 244.06	95 **Am** 243.06	96 **Cm** 247.07	97 **Bk** 247.07	98 **Cf** 251.08	99 **Es** 252.08	100 **Fm** 257.09	101 **Md** 258.09	102 **No** 258.10	103 **Lr** 260.10

3 GETTING THE MOST OUT OF CLASS

In a typical school year you spend an average of 800 hours in classes. *How* you spend that time will determine your academic success. This chapter focuses on using class time wisely.

IN THIS CHAPTER YOU WILL LEARN HOW TO:

- **prepare for class**
- **participate fully**
- **ask significant questions**
- **interpret a teacher's lecture**
- **take effective notes**

PREPARATION BEGINS AT HOME

You need to come to each class prepared to learn. Homework is the bridge from one day's class to the next. Keep a special assignment book. Get the phone numbers of one or two "serious" students early in the school year.

If you are absent or are not sure about what the assignment is, call one of those serious students for information. Do every assignment, including those that require only reading. Chapter Five has suggestions for using textbooks effectively.

Whether the assignment is to be read or written, note anything that you don't understand. Make a sincere effort to figure it out yourself; ask a parent or sibling; call a friend. If you are still con-

Be sure to come to class with everything you need.

fused, frame specific questions to ask in class the next day. Keep your homework and those questions in a special place, perhaps a separate pocket in your folder.

Always check your materials and pack your bookbag the night before. Be sure you have everything you need:

- homework
- textbooks, other required books
- notebooks, folders, paper
- pencils, pens, ruler, other supplies

Arrive in class as early as possible. This gives you time to choose your seat (if not assigned). Sit near the front if you can: You will see and hear better. There are also usually fewer distractions there. Wherever you sit, avoid the people who tend to distract you.

The minute or two before the bell is a time to get organized and mentally ready. Use this time to:

- get into a frame of mind for that class
- organize your materials—pen out, paper ready, book open
- look over previous assignments and notes

"Learning is not attained by chance, it must be sought for with ardor and attended to with diligence. "

—Abigail Adams,
wife of U.S. President John Adams

CLASS PARTICIPATION

Class participation is more than asking and answering questions. Your response depends on the nature of the class and what the class is doing on a given day. Most classes consist of a combination of teacher lecture or demonstrations, class discussion, and individual student or group activities.

Here are a few examples of class participation through assigned activities.

- *Lab work*. Teachers are usually clear about how students are to perform lab work. Keep those expectations in mind. Observe and record carefully. Do your part—don't unfairly rely on your lab partner. Clean up properly and on time.
- *Foreign language*. Learning a foreign language entails speaking it often. Volunteer in class: You'll become more proficient with practice, and the teacher's input will help you improve.
- *Group projects*. When class time is provided, use it wisely. There may be resources available that can be used only in the classroom. Neither your teacher nor your partners will appreciate wasted class time.

" Conversation is the laboratory and workshop of the student."

—Ralph Waldo Emerson, essayist

Your participation is most noticeable, of course, in class discussions. Here are five steps that will improve your contributions to class discussions.

MEMORY TRICK: PLTPS

Remember these five principles:

PREPARE. Keep up with assignments so you will have some knowledge and understanding of the current topic.

LISTEN. Pay attention to and think about what others are saying. See Chapter Three for active listening strategies.

THINK. Think about what you can say that will add to the discussion. Don't just echo what others have said. Don't be afraid to state a differing opinion, but be sure you have the facts to support your view.

PLAN. Plan what you want to say and how you want to say it. Say it to yourself. Make sure it sounds sensible.

SPEAK. Speak so that everyone can hear you, not just the teacher.

Questions are an appropriate part of class discussions. You shouldn't just sit there if you don't understand the issue or what an individual is saying about it. Here are some pointers about asking questions.

- Be prepared. Don't ask the teacher or a classmate to explain something you would know if you had done your homework. But if a homework assignment is confusing or subject to different interpretations, ask questions that will clarify it for you.

If you don't understand it, you are probably not the only one.

- Questions are a way to participate in the discussion when you are too shy to express your opinion. A well-timed and relevant question can keep the momentum of a discussion going.
- If the speaker is not making sense, a question can pinpoint the weakness. Your question should reflect what is clear and what is not: "I see A and B, but I don't understand C. Please explain that part again."
- Ask questions respectfully. Everyone deserves courtesy.

LECTURES ARE NOT A PASSIVE ACTIVITY

Even when the teacher is doing the talking, you need to be an active participant. It's not enough to let the words wash over you. Sit up. Put your mind in gear. Ask yourself questions: Do I understand? How does this relate to what I already know? See if you can draw any conclusions on your own. In other words, take charge of your learning.

If you do not understand something that is said, make a note to ask at an appropriate time. Waiting is often the best strategy because the point that confuses you may be explained a little later in the lecture. Keep in mind other suggestions made earlier in this chapter concerning questions.

As your teacher speaks, he or she will be providing clues to what is most important. Pay attention to voice inflection and body language. You will find these and other suggestions for active listening in Chapter Seven and in the section below.

NOTE TAKING

The most active thing you can do when anyone lectures is take notes. Note taking has many benefits:

- It helps you stay awake and alert.

Sit up and put your mind in gear. Even when the teacher is doing all the talking, you need to be an active participant.

- It enhances your ability to remember.
- It helps you organize information and ideas.
- It makes studying for tests easier.

In spite of these benefits, many students hate to take notes. They complain that the information is in the textbook anyway or that the teacher talks so fast that they can't keep up. The most likely problem is that the student doesn't know how to take notes. This chapter will provide specific directions on how to take notes. All you need to do is overcome your resistance to using this most important study tool.

Often teachers lecture on information that is not found in the textbook or the assigned readings. If this information seems significant, don't simply trust your memory; take detailed notes. If teachers do lecture on the contents of the assigned reading, they usually do so for good reasons:

- *To highlight the most important ideas and concepts.* You may be able to figure out what is most important on your own, but why not take advantage of your teacher's experience? And knowing what your teacher values may be a guide to what will appear on a test. Moreover, most teachers include at least one question in every test that can be answered only if you've been paying attention in class.

- *To explain material from the book that is difficult to understand.* Your teacher can give examples, draw diagrams, or make demonstrations that help you understand. Later refer to the notes you take (including copies of diagrams) to deepen your understanding.

HOW TO TAKE EFFECTIVE CLASS NOTES

Here are 5 simple points to remember:

1. Use a binder, folder, loose-leaf sheets of paper, and a pen or pencil.
2. Write the name of the class and date at the top of each sheet. Number the pages.
3. Take notes in a form that works for you. Leave extra space on each page.
4. Take notes only on what is important.
5. Review your notes and fill in later.

Now let's consider each in more detail.

1 USE A BINDER, FOLDER, LOOSE-LEAF SHEETS OF PAPER, AND A PEN.

A three-ring binder is the best place to store your notes. A binder with loose-leaf paper has more flexibility than does a spiral or fixed-page (composition style) notebook. With a binder it will be easy to

- remove the notes you don't need
- add handouts, quizzes, tests, and other information
- reorganize your notes as needed

This does not mean you need to carry a large heavy binder from class to class. In fact, all you need for class is a folder and a generous supply of loose-leaf paper. Travel light—leave your binder in your locker. An added advantage: If your folder is lost, you'll lose only one day's notes. The rest are safely stored in your binder.

2 WRITE THE NAME OF THE CLASS AND THE DATE AT THE TOP OF EACH SHEET. NUMBER THE PAGES.

It is important to identify each page and to number it. Your notes may fall on the floor, or otherwise get out of order. The information at the top of each sheet will make it easy to organize and sort your notes when it is time to put them in your binder.

3 TAKE NOTES IN A FORM THAT WORKS FOR YOU. LEAVE EXTRA SPACE ON EACH PAGE.

The most common form for note taking is the outline form. Students often fear this method because they find it difficult to maintain the "proper " form while quickly taking notes. Since notes are for you, don't worry about perfection. Become familiar with the outline, but don't be a slave to it.

OUTLINE FORM

TITLE OR TOPIC

I. First main idea

- **A. Major point: detail about the first main idea**
  - **1. Subpoint: detail about the major point**
    - **a. detail about the subpoint**
- **B. Major point: record detail about the first main idea**

II. Second main idea

Here is an example from a science lecture.

GLOBAL WARMING

I. Carbon dioxide traps heat in atmosphere

A. Release of CO_2 by human uses

1. gasoline in cars

2. coal-burning electrical power plants

3. clearing trees for farming

a. destruction of tropical rain forests

If you lose track of exactly where you are on the outline form, just put all the details that pertain to a particular point in an indented list under that point. Most people can easily do that kind of rough outline during the lecture. You can always add the letters and numbers later.

GRAPHIC ORGANIZERS AND DIAGRAMS

In some cases, it might be appropriate to map out the ideas covered in the lecture. A visual representation can show how the ideas are related. You can create your own form or use one shown below.

- *Web.* Put the main idea in a circle in the center of your paper. Put major points in circles around the main idea; use lines to connect major points to the main idea. Attach detail circles to the point they support. This is how it might look.

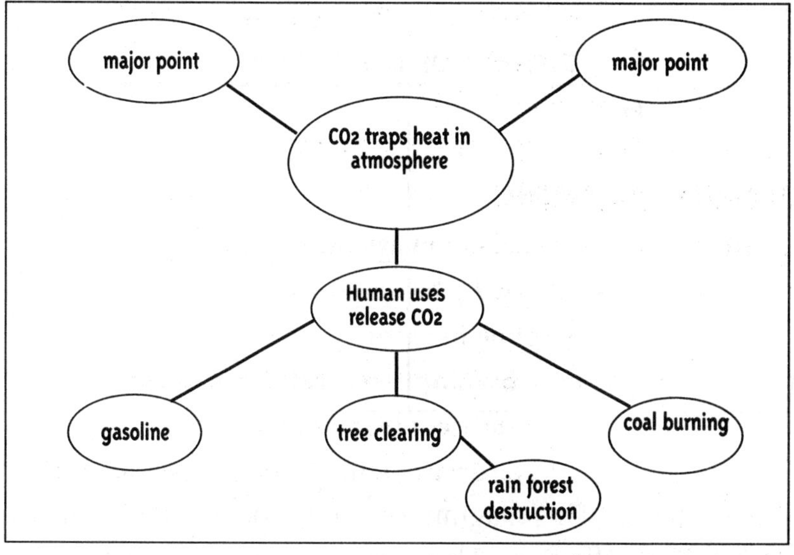

- *Tree.* In this pattern, the main idea is placed at the top of the page. Major points are on a line on the next level. Details that support them are on the next, and so on. The pattern ends up looking like a pine tree.

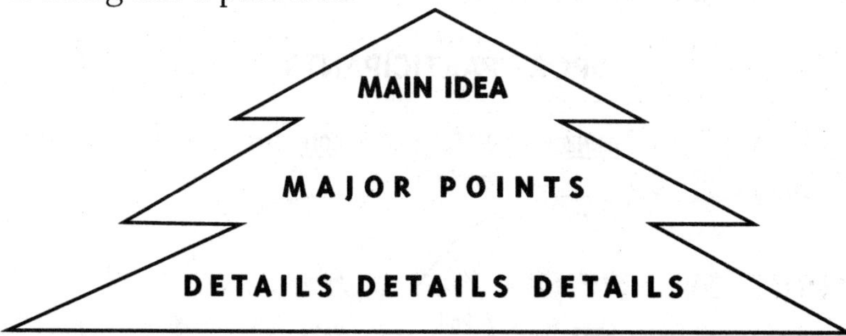

Diagrams and charts are very useful for showing relationships among ideas. They can be self-designed or standard patterns, such as the T-chart and the Venn diagram pictured on the next page.

- *T-charts.* This chart can be used to show two aspects of a topic, person, object, or event. The topic or item to be analyzed is written on the horizontal bar (top) of the T. The vertical line divides the two lists.

SUBJECT OF DISCUSSION	
PROS	**CONS**

- *Venn diagram.* This diagram uses interlocking circles in a way that is very effective. The outer portion of each circle contains elements that are different; the overlapping area contains the common or similar element. From the diagram below, you can see at a glance who plays both tennis and golf (Phil, Eric, and Sara).

SPORT PARTICIPANTS

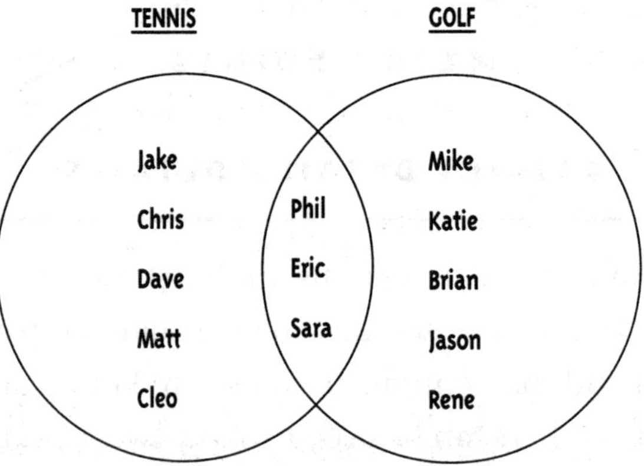

MAKING A LIST

In this method you jot down key words as they occur in the lecture. Write only the important words that relate to the main ideas and points you want to remember. Use a bullet (•) to signal each new entry. The listing method works well in a class that covers a lot of terms, events, names, and dates.

Next to each term, write a few words or phrases that relate to it: the definition or examples the teacher offers. Underline words or phrases for emphasis. Skip a few lines between each term. Here is how notes on the global warming topic might look in a list.

- global warming—carbon dioxide traps heat in atmosphere
- human use—cars, power plants, tree clearing = release of CO^2
- farming—destruction of rain forests

The goal of this method is to highlight the major ideas. When you review your notes later, you can use the skipped lines to add more detailed information from the textbook. One weakness of this method is that it does not show relationships clearly. Some students later use their lists to create an outline or word map to show how the ideas and details are related.

Good note takers use a variety of forms and methods. Their choices depend on the type of material being covered and the way in which it is being presented. They use the method or combination of methods that help them understand the material.

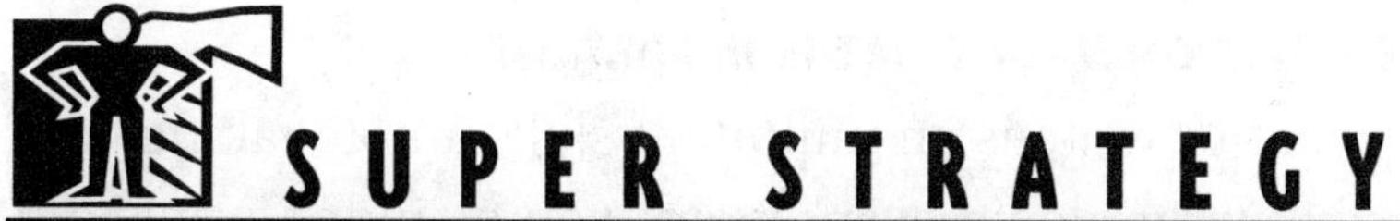

TAILOR YOUR METHOD TO EACH CLASS

Here are some suggestions for using each technique in particular classes as well as sample situations.

SOCIAL STUDIES

- Since social studies involves events, names, and dates, the listing method may be satisfactory.
- When the topic is complex, such as the causes of the Revolutionary War, the outline method would be more useful.
- To compare political platforms, use a T-chart.

SCIENCE AND HEALTH

- To compare the characteristics of reptiles and amphibians, use a Venn diagram.
- When a lecture is presenting a broad view of a topic, webbing or outlining would be better methods.
- During a lab, keep a list of key terms your teacher mentions.

ENGLISH AND LITERATURE

- When the lecture is about the characters in a novel, you might use a T-chart or other graphic organizer.
- When the lecture is about themes and sub-themes in Shakespearean plays, the outline form will allow you to record more detail.
- In a seminar (primarily student discussion), the more informal webbing or listing methods may work best. You can add to your notes later.

4 TAKE NOTES ONLY ON WHAT IS IMPORTANT

Knowing what to write is an important skill in note taking. You can't possibly write down every word; you wouldn't want to if you could. Your aim is to get the big picture. See the Thumbs Up/Thumbs Down feature on the next page for guidelines for selecting what to write.

TAKING NOTES: KNOW WHAT TO WRITE

THUMBS UP TO

- main points and concepts
- examples that deepen your understanding
- details that fit the "theme" of the lecture
- information that shows how concepts are connected
- anything repeated or emphasized by the teacher
- anything the teacher writes on the chalkboard

THUMBS DOWN TO

- word-by-word transcripts
- insignificant details
- basic information that you already know
- obvious examples; too many examples
- details that are irrelevant to the topic
- emphasis on form, rather than content

Teachers often give clues to what they feel is important. These clues are not always obvious. Review Chapter Seven for ways to read your teacher's body language. Below are some signals you should not ignore.

- *Verbal.* By repeating a word, a phrase, or an idea, your teacher indicates its importance. Tone of voice and volume are other indicators. Listen for words such as *first, significantly*, and *finally* and phrases such as *most of all, in summary*, and *don't forget*. Pauses should also put you on alert.
- *Nonverbal.* Watch your teacher for signals: raising the eyebrows, tapping the desk or board, or other hand gestures. Learn to read these and other signals—these attention-getters tell you it's time to write.

"Your teacher can lead you to the door: the acquiring of learning rests with each person."
—Chinese proverb

5 REVIEW AND FILL IN LATER

Most students don't look at their notes until it is time to study for a quiz or test. That is a mistake. Successful students read over their notes often—every evening, every few days, or at least at the end of every week. It will take only a few minutes per subject if you do it often, and the benefits are enormous.

- *You can fill and fix.* While the lecture is still fresh in your mind, you can catch and fix any mistakes in your notes. If you are worried that a word, phrase, or concept will not be clear later, fill in as necessary.
- *You can elaborate on your notes.* Add information in extra spaces such as margins and skipped lines. In fact, some students write only on the front of the sheet in class—they fill the back with more information from memory, the textbook, or other sources.
- *You can discover and indicate relationships.* It is important to note any relationships among the people, events, and concepts discussed in the lecture. It will probably be obvious to you right after the lecture. It may *not* be next month.
- *You become aware of major themes and ideas.* When you come back to your notes with a fresh eye, you are more likely to notice the big picture. Some students are able to capture the theme during the lecture and jot it down before leaving class. This second look is important for those who can't.
- *You can highlight as you review.* You may wish to highlight or underline what is most important. This will help you remem-

ber it. You'll get more out of any future lectures on the topic, and you'll benefit at test studying time too.

SUPER TACTICS

GETTING THE MOST OUT OF MATH CLASS

Your class time is critically important because it is difficult to teach yourself math from a textbook. Your success in math will depend on proper class preparation, participation, and note taking.

PREPARATION

It is entirely too easy to fall behind in math since each concept builds on the previous one. What you learn one day will become the basis for learning the next. It is essential to do the assigned homework to be sure that you truly understand the principles that have been taught in class. Make the effort to logically *reason* your way through your homework. It is not enough to simply manipulate the numbers in a copycat manner. Here are some critical thinking approaches that will maximize your learning.

- **Examine the sample problems carefully. Identify the type of problem, think about what information you have and what information you need, decide which procedure or strategy will solve the problem.**
- **Understand how and why a mathematical process works. If possible, relate the problem to something real in your life.**
- **Talk your way through a difficult or new kind of problem. Verbalizing helps keep you on track and builds your awareness of relationships.**
- **Once you have an answer, look back. Is your answer reasonable? If not, check your figures and rethink the procedure. Try again.**

CLASS PARTICIPATION

In elementary school, you often worked problems on the chalkboard. As you progress in your math education, boardwork becomes less common. But this does not mean that you sit passively in class while your teacher presents new material. Learning math is an active process; take advantage of every opportunity to become involved.

While your teacher is working a problem on the chalkboard, do the problem at your seat. Try to recognize how the problem relates to something you already know. See if you can choose a strategy to solve the problem. As the teacher works, don't just watch—think how each step leads to the next.

If you are working in a group, pay attention to the strategies the other students use. Ask them to verbalize what they are doing and why. Don't be afraid to suggest alternative strategies; try some of the following:

- restate the problem
- look for a pattern
- make a diagram
- make a chart or list
- work backward
- guess and check

NOTE TAKING IN MATH CLASS

Since math is a number-based subject, you may think you do not need to take notes. In fact, taking notes should be part of every math class. In addition to the suggestions on note taking earlier in this chapter, the tips below can make your note taking in math class more effective.

- *Copy everything exactly.* Your teacher will be writing theorems, rules, definitions, diagrams, and examples on the chalkboard. Don't change, shorten, or leave anything out. Leave extra room around any sample problems you copy. Verify formulas, etc. later by reviewing your textbook.
- *Include any explanations the teacher gives about a problem or procedure.* Label everything. Use arrows to connect the expla-

nation with the proper part of the problem. Be sure you understand how and why the procedure solves the problem.

- *Make note of any patterns you discover.* Sometimes many problems follow the same pattern. But don't be fooled—think about each problem individually.
- *When you are assigned problems to do on your own or in a group, keep complete notes on your work.* Don't just solve the problems; next to each example, state the reasoning used to solve it.
- *Be neat. Accuracy is crucial in math.* Look over your notes and revise or recopy any that are unclear. Keep them orderly in your binder so that you can refer to them when doing homework and reviewing for tests and quizzes.

FOR REVIEW

1. How can you prepare for class?
2. What are five steps for improving your contributions to class discussions?
3. How do you ask appropriate questions in class?
4. What are some of the benefits of taking notes?
5. What are the five points for taking effective class notes?
6. Describe three different methods of taking notes.
7. How do you know what is important to write in your notes?
8. Why should you review and revise your notes often?

ORDER OF OPERATIONS

There is a proper order in which to perform operations within a problem.

Memorize the following to help you:

Please **R**emember **M**y **D**ear **A**unt **S**ue.

P - parentheses
R - roots and powers
M - multiplication
D - division
A - addition
S - subtraction

SAMPLE PROBLEM:

$2^2 \times (3 + 4) + (2 \times 5) = ?$

		$(3 + 4)$		(2×5)	
P		**7**		**10**	
	2^2	$\times$ 7	+	10	
R	**4**				
	4	$\times$ 7	+	10	
M		**28**	+	10	
D		N/A			
A		28	+	10	= 38
S		N/A			

ROMAN NUMERALS

I	1	**I**	1	**VIII**	8	**CCC**	300
V	5	**II**	2	**IX**	9	**CD**	400
X	10	**III**	3	**X**	10	**DCC**	700
L	50	**IV**	4	**XX**	20	**CM**	900
C	100	**V**	5	**XL**	40	**MC**	1100
D	500	**VI**	6	**LXX**	70	**MCM**	1900
M	1000	**VII**	7	**XC**	90	**MM**	2000

UNITS OF MEASURE

English		Metric equivalent
foot (ft)	= 12 inches (in)	30.480 centimeters (cm)
yard (yd)	= 3 ft = 36 in	0.914 meters (m)
mile (mi)	= 1760 yd = 5280 ft	1.609 kilometers (km)
square ft	= 144 square in	0.093 square meters
square yd	= 9 square ft	0.836 square meters
acre	= 4840 square yd	4047 square meters
square mi	= 640 acres	2.590 square kilometers
tablespoon (T)	= 3 teaspoons (t)	14.786 mililiters (ml)
cup (c)	= 16 T = 8 fluid ounces (fl oz)	236.584 mililiters
pint (pt)	= 2 cups	0.473 liters (l)
quart (qt)	= 2 pt = 4 c = 32 fl oz	0.946 liters
gallon (gal)	= 4 quarts	3.785 liters

FRACTIONS

Addition and subtraction: denominators must be the same

Example: $\frac{5}{12} + \frac{4}{18}$

First find the **lowest common denominator** of 12 and 18:

1. factor each denominator $12 = 2 \times 2 \times 3$
   $18 = 2 \times 3 \times 3$
2. circle the factors they have in common $12 = 2 \times 3 \times 2$
   $18 = 2 \times 3 \times 3$
3. multiply the common factors: $2 \times 3 = 6$
4. multiply this by any additional factors: $6 \times \mathbf{2} \times \mathbf{3} = 36$

Next convert each fraction to an equivalent fraction with the common denominator 36 and add:

$$\frac{5}{12} = \frac{\mathbf{15}}{36}$$

$$\frac{4}{18} = \frac{\mathbf{8}}{36}$$

$$\frac{\mathbf{23}}{36}$$

Multiplication - multiply numerators and multiply denominators

Example: $\frac{2}{3} \times \frac{4}{5} = \frac{2 \times 4}{3 \times 5} = \frac{8}{15}$

Division - invert the second fraction and multiply

Example: $\frac{2}{7} \div \frac{1}{3} = \frac{2}{7} \times \frac{3}{1} = \frac{6}{7}$

ALGEBRA

Operation Properties

1. Associative property of addition: $a + (b + c) = (a + b) + c$
2. Associative property of multiplication: $a(bc) = (ab)c$
3. Commutative property of addition: $a + b = b + a$
4. Commutative property of multiplication: $ab = ba$
5. Distributive property of multiplication over addition: $a(b + c) = ab + ac$
6. Distributive property of multiplication over subtraction: $a(b - c) = ab - ac$

Factoring

$a + 2ab + b^2 = (a + b)^2$

$a^2 - 2ab + b^2 = (a - b)^2$

$a^2 - b^2 = (a - b)(a + b)$

$ac + ad + bc + bd = (a + b)(c + d)$

$a^2 + ac + ab + bc = (a + b)(a + c)$

GEOMETRIC FORMULAS

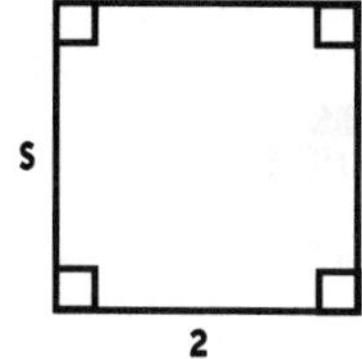

SQUARE

Area: $A=s^2$

RECTANGLE

Area: $A = l \times w$

Perimeter: $P = 2 \times (l + w)$

PARELLELOGRAM

Area: $A=bh$

TRIANGLE

Area: $A=\frac{bh}{2}$

CIRCLE

Area: $A=\pi r^2$

Circumference: $C= \pi d = 2\pi r$

RIGHT CYLINDER

Volume: $V=\pi r^2 h$

SUPPPLEMENTARY ANGLES

Supplementary angles add up to 180°

COMPLEMENTARY ANGLES

Complementary angles add up to 90°

PYTHAGOREAN THEOREM

$a^2 + b^2 = c^2$

4 WRITING WITH A PURPOSE

Writing enables you to communicate your ideas and reach a large number of people in all kinds of places through reports, letters, books, and articles. Unfortunately, no one can understand what you're trying to say unless your ideas are expressed clearly and precisely. Your ideas must be well thought out or they won't make sense, no matter how hard you try to write them. Good writing is based on clear thinking. If your thoughts are vague and muddy, that will be reflected in what you write. Remember, people evaluate the way you think by how well you write.

IN THIS CHAPTER, YOU'LL LEARN HOW TO:

- **develop a theme, or message, in your writing**
- **analyze your audience and write for them**
- **create an effective opening paragraph**
- **use a visual style of writing**
- **make sure your writing is clear and simple**
- **use writing skills to develop an English essay**

WHAT'S YOUR POINT?

Jeffrey looked at the paper his teacher had just handed back to him and let out a loud groan. At the top right-hand corner was a grade Jeffrey had hoped wouldn't be there: C-. And next to it, the teacher had written: "I couldn't figure out your main point. What are you trying to tell me about your topic?"

Most writing projects in school begin with a topic—either you pick one yourself or the teacher assigns one to you. Perhaps it's the Battle of Gettysburg, or Shakespeare's Macbeth or the nesting habits of birds. These are huge topics, and there are lots of things you could say about each one—far too much for the average composition. So you must decide what your main point or message about the topic is going to be. This message is called the theme. Your theme might be that General Robert E. Lee should not have launched Pickett's Charge on the third day of the Battle of Gettysburg, or that Shakespeare's Macbeth proves too much ambition is a dangerous thing.

"A theme captures in just a few words or sentences—in other words a theme summarizes—what it is you want to say about the subject at hand."

—Herbert and Jill Meyer, writers

DEVELOPING YOUR THEME

The next time you're trying to develop a theme for a writing project, here are several things to keep in mind.

1. *The theme is not the same as the subject.* The theme is the point you want to make about the subject—the message you want to deliver about it.

2. *Every successful piece of writing has a theme.* All your ideas should be organized around the central theme. The theme acts as the spine of your paper, and everything you write should relate to the theme.

3. *The first step in any writing assignment is to decide on a theme, then jot it down.* You should be able to state the thesis in one or two sentences. If it takes more, you probably aren't too clear about what the theme should be.

4. *Sometimes a topic that you're assigned may seem boring. Try to find a theme that's interesting so you can bring the topic to life.* For example, the nesting habits of birds might not be a subject that excites you. But if you can relate this subject to a personal experience, it might make your writing assignment far more interesting. Your theme might be how the robin in your backyard taught you about home building.

WHY ARE YOU WRITING?

Writing can accomplish different things. Some types of writing *explain.* In science, for example, you might write up an experiment by explaining the process you followed to test a scientific theory. Or in history, you might explain how a bill is approved in Congress. If you work part time at a store after school, you might be asked by your boss to write down the steps for receiving merchandise so new employees will know exactly how to do it. Whenever you have to explain something, it's important to make sure that your writing is easy to understand and that all the information is presented in the proper sequence so there's no confusion.

Some types of writing *describe.* You might describe a warm summer day in the countryside or the cold, dark rooms in a rambling

Whenever you have to explain something, make sure that all the information is presented in the proper sequence so there's no confusion.

old house. Vivid descriptions depend on choosing adjectives, adverbs, and other descriptive words that bring a scene to life so your readers can see it. Writers often try to present details in a specific order. For example, they might start at the front of a room, where the reader would enter, and work toward the back.

A great deal of what is written is designed to *persuade*. You may try to convince the reader of your point of view or prod the reader to take action. Perhaps you're writing a letter to the editor of the local newspaper expressing your opinion on whether a new recreation center should be built in your community or whether school should be in session all year. In this type of writing, it's important to select powerful arguments that support your viewpoint and present them with as much evidence as you can muster.

Many projects combine these types of writing: explanation, description, and persuasion. For example, a travel writer might try to persuade people to vacation at a new beach resort by describing the wonderful activities available there and explaining—step by step—the directions for getting to the resort.

ANALYZE YOUR AUDIENCE

Almost everything you write is designed to be read by someone else. If you want to have impact, you'd better understand your reader.

- *Find out what the reader knows about your subject and theme.* Never assume that the reader already understands something so you don't have to explain it. If anything, err in the direction of providing too much explanation rather than too little.
- *Use language that fits what the reader expects.* If your teacher has assigned you a formal report, avoid slang expressions. These will only detract from the impression that you're trying to make on the reader. However, if you're writing a short story that includes dialogue, slang might be appropriate.
- *Put yourself in the reader's place.* Ask yourself; What do my readers want to know? What will interest the reader? What does the reader really care about? The answers to these questions should guide what you decide to include in your paper.

THE FIRST PARAGRAPH

There's an old saying that "first impressions are lasting impressions." Certainly, the first paragraph of a report is more important by far than any other paragraph that follows. In the first paragraph, you should present your theme so the reader will know what point you're trying to make. The theme, or message, goes first, then all the other points and details follow in later paragraphs. This is called the pyramid style of writing. It's similar to the way most newspaper articles are written. The headline, or title, comes at the top, followed by a paragraph that tells the most important information. Then the other points come later.

PYRAMID STYLE OF WRITING

THEME
IMPORTANT DETAILS
OTHER POINTS

You could begin your first paragraph with words such as "In this report, my theme will be...." But that's a pretty boring way to start. The reader might fall asleep before he or she even gets started! If you want to grab the reader's attention, you have to put yourself in his or her place and write a powerful opening paragraph.

WRITING A POWERFUL OPENING PARAGRAPH

Here are a few suggestions that will make the reader sit up and take notice when he or she begins your composition.

- **<u>Begin with a story that illustrates the theme of your paper.</u> If you're writing a biography, for example, start with an interesting anecdote from the person's life.**
- **<u>Open with a personal experience.</u> Perhaps something has happened to you that will drive home your main point to the reader. This will personalize your writing and make a huge impact on the reader.**
- **<u>Lead with a report from the media.</u> Something that you saw on television or read in a magazine may have seemed especially interesting. That event can be another effective way to introduce your theme in the opening paragraph. You may want to begin a file of articles that you can use for future writing assignments.**
- **<u>Talk to your friends.</u> Tell them about the theme of your paper.**

Perhaps someone you know has an interesting story that will work as an opening for your project.

- Tell the reader something he or she doesn't know. Many writers start with the obvious—information the reader is likely to have seen or heard before. Try to find an interesting fact or statistic that the reader will find new.
- You don't need to begin at the beginning. Writers often start at the top—the beginning of a historical process or the earliest years of a person's life. But frequently the most interesting story comes later. Start your first paragraph there. That way, you'll hook the reader and he or she will want to read further. In later paragraphs, you can double back and pick up the story at the beginning.
- Draw a word picture. A descriptive opening that allows the reader to visualize a scene can be very effective because it makes the reader feel as if he or she is seeing the story unfold in person.
- Don't forget the teacher. Your teacher may be the only one who reads what you've written. But he or she is human, too. Teachers are forced to read a lot of boring material. The more interesting your work, the more inclined the teacher will be to thank you and to grade your paper highly.

"Beginnings are important."

—John Irving, writer

IT'S ALL IN THE DETAILS

When they appear in court, lawyers rely on evidence to prove their case. They try to support every argument with convincing information that will be persuasive to a jury. When you write, you need evidence to support your main ideas. Your opinions

Evaluate what you read and make sure the author is an expert in the field.

aren't enough. The main idea is like the top of a pyramid. If it isn't supported by solid rock, it will fall. Accurate data provide the building blocks on which your ideas must rest. Where do you find the data? In books and articles, most of which will probably be stored in your library. Or you can check out what's on the Web. These sources provide interesting quotes, stories, statistics, and other information that can be utilized for your writing project. A note of caution: Evaluate what you read and make sure the author is an expert in the field. Usually his or her credentials are included on the inside back cover of a book or at the end of an article in a magazine. You have to be especially careful when using Internet sources since absolutely anyone can put up a Web page. It's a lot more difficult and expensive to publish and distribute a book, which weeds out a lot of the trash!

If you decide to quote from one of these sources, make sure you indicate in the body of the paper—or in a footnote at the end—where you found the quotation. Otherwise you may be guilty of *plagiarism* (using someone else's words and representing them as your own).

RULES OF EVIDENCE

THUMBS UP if you:

Check the validity of your sources and make sure that the authors are experts in their fields.

Use the exact words found in a source, put them in quotation marks, and indicate where you found them.

Try to find more evidence that will support one of them, when two sources disagree.

THUMBS DOWN if you:

Think every source is valuable as long as it supports your theme.

Use another author's exact words without giving that person credit in your report.

Don't worry if sources disagree, just take a guess on which one might be correct.

THE VISUAL STYLE OF WRITING

Writing is a visual experience. As readers look at the printed page, they are struck visually by what they see. If you've written long blocks of type that fill the entire page, the reader is apt to be put off. Who wants to read sentence after sentence without a break? Instead, it's easier for a reader to look at a short paragraph, digest the ideas presented, then take a breath before moving on to the next paragraph. Headings and subheadings help too. They break up the type and signal the reader that you, the writer, are introducing something new. This book uses headings and subheadings quite a bit to make each page more visually interesting.

This book also relies on other visual devices. Some pages have charts and boxes. Information is bulleted. If you use a computer, it's easy to create these types of visual elements. In addition, you can set off words in boldface or italics to give them emphasis in your writing.

Each of these techniques adds visual interest. Don't forget, we live in a visual society. Much of the information we receive comes via television or over the Internet. People expect to be visually stimulated by what they see. Visual interest holds the reader's attention and prevents the reader from mentally tuning out and not finishing what you have written. Anything you can do to make the printed page visually exciting will more likely keep the reader involved.

KEEP IT SIMPLE

Once you've finished work on a writing project, let it sit for a day or so. Then go back and look at it again. (This is a good reason not to wait until the last minute to get started on a writing assignment!) Here are a few guidelines to keep in mind as you go over what you've written.

1. *Make it concise.* Charles Dickens may have been paid by the word, but you aren't. Readers will thank you for making what you write as short as possible. But, you ask, the teacher wants me to write a ten-page paper, so don't I have to carry out the assignment? Yes, but not by resorting to needless padding to present your thoughts. Add more ideas, not more words, to make your paper effective and to complete the ten-page assignment.
2. *Keep it simple.* Some writers like to use "high-brow" words and long sentences. They think these things impress their readers. They don't. Most readers prefer simple words and brief, easy-to-read sentences.
3. *Read the paper aloud.* Reading is not only a visual experience, it's an auditory one too. As the reader looks at what you've written, he or she is saying the words silently and hearing

The spellcheck function on your computer can take you only so far. You may have used the wrong word, but the computer won't catch it if it's spelled correctly.

them in his or her ears. If any sentences sound awkward, the reader may be distracted by your words and not pay attention to your ideas. If you run out of breath before you get to the end of a sentence, chances are your reader will too. Take out some of the words and shorten the sentence so your reader will be able to follow your paper more easily.

4. *Make sure it's correct.* There's nothing that looks worse on the printed page than a misspelled word or an incorrect punctuation mark. It reflects badly on you. Your reader may think that if you've made this type of mistake, there may also be errors in the information you've presented. If you use a computer, your software may include a spellcheck function that can help you spot errors in spelling. But the computer can take you only so far. You may have used the wrong word, but the computer won't catch it if it's spelled correctly. For example, you might have written *principle* when you meant *principal.* The best way to find these mistakes is to make a hard copy and proofread it. Don't proofread on the computer screen. You'll miss too much that way. And if you aren't sure whether the word is right, use a dictionary.

MEMORY TRICK:

M A C E

Whenever you write, remember these four principles:

Message or theme should be easy to understand.

Audience Appeal should be part of your writing. Hook your readers in the first paragraph and keep them involved throughout your composition.

Clear, simple language is essential. Make your words and sentences easy to follow.

Error free is your goal. Proofread to ensure that there are no misspelled words or mistakes in punctuation.

SUPER TACTIC

WRITING IN LANGUAGE ARTS

In language arts, you have an opportunity to read many different kinds of literature. These include short stories, novels, plays, and poetry that have been created by some of the world's great writers.

- **A SHORT STORY is, as its name suggests, a short piece of fiction. There is usually a single story line, or plot, and only a few characters. The author may even restrict the action to a single location, keeping the story as tight as possible.**
- **A NOVEL is a longer piece of fiction. There may be several main characters as well as a large number of minor characters. The**

author often weaves together a main plot along with several subplots that occur in a variety of locations. All of these elements are designed to maintain the reader's interest throughout the entire work.

- A PLAY is designed to be seen and heard, unlike the novel and short story, which are written to be read. All the action occurs on a stage and may involve a single plot with only two characters in one setting or a large cast of actors, major and minor plots, and numerous scene changes. Since plays are written to be performed in front of an audience, the author—called a *playwright*—includes directions for the actors. These tell the actors what their actions should be as they deliver their lines (e.g. walk to the center of the stage, or draw your sword).
- A POEM communicates an author's experience or feelings or thoughts. Although some poets write long epics—Homer's Odyssey, for example—most poems are much shorter works. Poems are often divided into groups of lines, called *stanzas.* And some of these lines may rhyme, although many modern poems do not use rhyming.

You have probably written book reviews and read them in newspapers and magazines. Reviews focus on a particular work of literature and describe all of its important elements—plot, characters, etc. As a reviewer, you are expected to evaluate the work, giving an opinion of whether the author wrote a worthwhile piece of literature and whether one should spend time reading it.

In high school, your English teacher will probably want you to write something different than a book review. Instead, your assignment may be to select a particular element of a literary work and analyze it in a report.

"For a man to write well, there are required three necessaries—to read the best authors, observe the best speakers, and much exercise of his own style."

—Ben Jonson, writer

ELEMENTS OF LITERATURE

Generally speaking, there are five elements that can be analyzed in a work of literature.

- **Plot.** The plot usually involves a conflict or problem that pits the characters against one another. The plot generally moves along to a climax, or high point in the action. Afterward, the problem is resolved. As you analyze the plot, ask yourself these questions:

  1. Is the conflict realistic?
  2. How well does the author move the plot along? Does it hold your interest?
  3. How realistic is the resolution of the problem?

- **Characters.** An author speaks to us through the characters. They act out the plot of the story. As you evaluate the characters, think about the following questions:

  1. Are the characters one-dimensional, or do they have many facets to them? In other words, do they seem like real people?
  2. Do their actions seem to flow naturally from their personalities?
  3. How natural does their dialogue sound?
  4. Do I care about what happens to the characters in the story?

- **Theme.** The concept of theme was discussed earlier in this chapter. Many authors try to communicate a message through their works. Ask yourself the following:

1. If the author has a theme, what is it?
2. How clearly is the theme expressed by the author? Do you agree or disagree with it?
3. How does the author support the theme through the plot and the characters?

• **Setting.** The setting is not only the place where the story occurs but also the time. Historical novels, for example, take place in the past; and science fiction is set in the future. As you think about the setting, ask yourself:

1. How well does the author depict the setting of the story?
2. Are all of the details accurate?
3. Does the setting seem to fit the plot, the theme, and the characters?

• **Language.** Good writers know how to use language effectively to communicate their ideas. By reading what they write, it can help you improve the way you use words in your writing. Think about these questions, as you evaluate the author's use of language:

1. Does the writer use figurative language, such as metaphors, similes, and symbols?
2. How well does the author use language to depict a setting or describe a character?
3. Is the author's language easy to understand or difficult to follow?

WRITING AN ESSAY IN SIX EASY STEPS

Understanding the various elements that make up a literary work will help you think of topics for an essay. You should follow a six-step process for writing your paper. These same steps apply whether you're writing a paper for English class or for one of your other classes.

1. *Narrow your topic; define your message.* Suppose you decide to focus on the characters in Shakespeare's *Hamlet.* Obviously, this is a huge topic—much too big for an essay. You must narrow the topic by deciding which character you want to write about and what message about him or her you want to communicate to your reader.
2. *Brainstorm ideas.* Spend some time thinking about all the ideas that seem related to your topic and message, then jot them down. Don't worry if some of the ideas appear foolish, include them anyway. Later, go back and begin to eliminate those that seem irrelevant to your paper. Group similar ideas under specific headings and think about the order in which you want to present all of the information in your paper. This organization of ideas will form a preliminary, informal outline for your writing project.
3. *Develop your evidence.* Carefully re-read the play *Hamlet* and look for evidence to support the ideas in your outline. You might also decide to consult several sources in the library. As you read, take notes. For this task, you can use index cards or write down the information in a notebook. The cards may be more flexible because you can arrange them in any order. This will enable you to organize and reorganize ideas later if you decide to change your outline. Be sure to leave space for a heading at the top of each card—the heading should correspond to one of the topics on your outline. The notes on each card should relate to this heading. By the way, if you're quoting material directly from a source, be sure to indicate the quotation on the card.

Look for evidence to support the ideas in your outline. As you read, take notes.

4. *Develop a final outline.* After you've finished taking notes, look them over carefully to make sure that you have enough information under each heading. During the research process, you may have discovered some new ideas that are relevant to your topic. These can be added to your outline. Finalize your outline, rearranging the order of ideas if necessary. Then organize your cards according to the sequence of ideas in the outline. Your final outline, together with the index cards, will provide the blueprint for writing your paper.
5. *Write the paper.* For the opening, begin with an interesting quote. This should be something that will immediately grab the attention of the reader and effectively communicate your message. In the body of the paper, develop each main heading in your outline with the information from your notes. Don't be afraid to consult your sources again, if you need to add another quote or example that's not in your notes. Sometimes more information is necessary to bring ideas fully to life for the reader. In the conclusion of the paper, restate the message and

try to illustrate it with another interesting example or anecdote. Remember, this is the last opportunity you have to make an impact on the reader, so you want to make it as powerful as possible.

6. *Revise the paper*. Don't try to revise the paper as soon as you finish it. By letting the paper sit for a while, you will return to it with a fresh eye and a different perspective. This will enable you to see problems that may not have been obvious earlier. First, read through each section to make sure that all the information fits logically together and that you have not left out any important points. Next, read the paper aloud. This will help you determine how well the words and sentences sound together. Finally, look through the paper a third time for any errors in grammar, punctuation, or spelling.

The author F. Scott Fitzgerald revised his novels over and over again until he was finally satisfied and ready to have them published.

By following these six steps, you can write more effectively. They will not only enable you to derive more satisfaction from writing, you'll also improve your grades in English and in other courses. In addition, you'll achieve greater success on a job where communication skills are an essential key to advancement. As a good writer, you'll be able to organize your ideas logically and present them in clear, powerful language. This will enable you to make your point and persuade others to follow you.

FOR REVIEW

1. What is the theme of a writing project? How does it differ from the topic?
2. What are three different purposes you can accomplish in your writing?
3. How do you analyze your readers and write for them?
4. What is the pyramid style of writing?
5. How do you write a first paragraph that grabs the interest of your readers?
6. What is the visual style of writing?
7. What are five major elements of literature?
8. What are the six steps in writing an English essay?

PUNCTUATION RULES

1. END MARKS

Use a period to end a complete statement. *She is a member of the team. They are going to a concert on Wednesday.*

Use a question mark to end a question. *Are you going to the dance? What is your dog's name?*

Use an exclamation point to end a statement that expresses strong feeling. *Don't be late! Finish what you're doing, now!*

2. COMMAS

Use a comma to punctuate words and phrases used in a series. *The long, narrow, winding road led to a rundown house. The celebration featured singers, dancers, and jugglers.* (Note: A comma before the *and* is optional. But be consistent!)

Use a comma after an introductory phrase or clause. *If we have a severe snow storm tonight, school will be canceled tomorrow.*

Use a comma before a coordinating conjunction, like *and* or *but,* to join two independent clauses.

The dog began to bark, and Sheila ran to the door to answer the bell.

3. SEMICOLONS

Use a semicolon to join two independent clauses, when you omit a coordinating conjunction. *Bill won the history award; Carol was given the composition prize.*

4. COLONS

When a list is given, it is often introduced with a colon. *We are offering three sports this fall: football, soccer, and field hockey.*

5. APOSTROPHES

Use apostrophes to indicate a missing letter in a contraction or to indicate possession. *Can't you find the way to Karen's house by using this map?*

6. QUOTATION MARKS

Use quotation marks around someone's exact words. *"Let's go to the park this afternoon," she said.*

SPELLING RULES

1. When adding *ness* and *ly* to a word, the word itself doesn't change.
Mean meanness final finally

2. Use *ie* when the sound is the long *e* sound, except after *c*. belief, relief, thief conceive, perceive, receive
Exceptions: either, neither, seize
Use *ei* when these two letters don't sound like the long *e*, or if they sound like long *a*. weight, freight, height.
Exceptions: friend, conscience

3. If a word ends in *e*, drop the *e* before adding a suffix that begins with a vowel. have having move moving rave raving leave leaving
Exceptions: Words that end in *ce* or *ge* with suffixes *able* and *ous:* notice noticeable courage courageous

4. When a word ends in a consonant followed by *y*, change the *y* to *i*, before adding a suffix unless the suffix itself begins with *i*.
duty dutiful fancy fanciful fortify fortifying clarify clarifying

5. Nouns ending in *s, sh, ch, z,* and *x* form plurals by adding *es*.
grass grasses fish fishes watch watches waltz waltzes box boxes

6. Nouns ending in a *y* preceded by a consonant form the plural by changing the *y* to *i* and adding *es*. If the *y* is preceded by a vowel, the plural is formed by adding *s*. duty duties puppy puppies day days journey journeys

COMMONLY MISUSED WORDS

Word	Meaning	Example
accept	to receive	I will accept your resignation.
except	left out	Leave all the furniture, except this chair.
affect	to have an impact	This will affect the way we do business.
effect	power to cause results	It had a tremendous effect on our lives.
ascent	a climb	She had a long ascent to the top of the mountain.
assent	approval	The principal gave her assent to our proposal.
break	shatter	I saw him break the glass.
brake	a device to stop a vehicle	The brakes in her car failed.
course	path of action; subject in school; part of a meal	History was her hardest course.
coarse	crude	He used coarse manners at dinner.
complement	to complete, make whole	We need a photographer to complement the staff.
compliment	praise	Carol received many compliments on her speech.
moral	the lesson of a story	The moral of that story is powerful.
morale	mental state	The morale of the team was very low.
peace	absence of war	The treaty brought peace to Europe.
piece	part of something	Give me a piece of bread.
principal	head of a school; most important	The principal is new this year.
principle	rule	I believe in the principle that honesty is the best policy.
route	a way to go	This is the long route to my school.
rout	flight; put to flight	The army was routed in the war.
than	in comparison with	This book is cheaper than that one.
then	afterward	Then he began to do his homework.

there	at that place	We'll put it there, in the corner.
their	belonging to them	Their house is near the school.
they're	contraction of they are	They're the best in the field.
weather	conditions outside	The weather is very stormy today.
whether	introduces alternatives	Let's decide whether to go this way or that way.
your	belonging to you	This is your problem.
you're	contraction of you are	You're not running fast enough.

COMMONLY MISSPELLED WORDS

accidentally	chorus	immediately	podium
accident	cinema	incredible	pompous
accurate	cliche	infallible	questionnaire
acquaintance	debris	interpret	ramshackle
agreeable	debut	integrity	raspberry
annihilate	desirable	laboratory	raucous
anniversary	disappear	languid	reciprocate
apologize	disguise	leisure	rhythm
appreciate	edible	likelihood	rogue
architect	efficient	lunatic	separate
arctic	environment	maintenance	sergeant
athletics	equipped	malign	simile
audience	especially	metaphor	souvenir
awkward	essential	municipal	sovereign
banana	existence	mysterious	spontaneous
bargain	fallacy	neighbor	synonym
belief	foreign	noxious	technical
bicycle	grammar	nozzle	temperature
bureaucracy	guarantee	omitted	theorem
calendar	gymnasium	opportunity	tragedy
cemetery	handkerchief	orchid	unanimous
ceremony	habitat	parliament	unnoticed
chieftan	harass	patient	vanquish
cocoon	helicopter	pedestal	vengeance
condemn	heresy	persnickety	vicinity
conscience	hospital	phantom	villain
chimpanzee	hygiene	pneumonia	wharf

COMMON IRREGULAR VERBS

Present	Past	Past Participle
be	was, were	(have) been
become	became	(have) become
begin	began	(have) begun
blow	blew	(have) blown
break	broke	(have) broken
bring	brought	(have) brought
catch	caught	(have) caught
come	came	(have) come
choose	chose	(have) chosen
do	did	(have) done
draw	drew	(have) drawn
drink	drank	(have) drunk
drive	drove	(have) driven
eat	ate	(have) eaten
fall	fell	(have) fallen
fight	fought	(have) fought
fly	flew	(have) flown
forget	forgot	(have) forgotten
freeze	froze	(have) frozen
get	got	(have) gotten
give	gave	(have) given
go	went	(have) gone
know	knew	(have) known
lay	laid	(have) laid
lead	led	(have) led
lie	lay	(have) lain
ride	rode	(have) ridden
ring	rang	(have) rung
rise	rose	(have) risen
see	saw	(have) seen
seek	sought	(have) sought
shake	shook	(have) shaken
speak	spoke	(have) spoken

Present	Past	Past Participle
steal	stole	(have) stolen
swim	swam	(have) swum
take	took	(have) taken
throw	threw	(have) thrown
wear	wore	(have) worn
write	wrote	(have) written

5 EFFECTIVE READING

A typical textbook contains between 50,000 and 100,000 words. Add to this stories, articles, and other outside reading you are assigned. Multiply that by the number of courses you are taking. The total is overwhelming, unless you have efficient, effective, and dependable techniques for tackling your reading assignments.

THIS CHAPTER WILL SHOW YOU HOW TO:

- **arrange a good reading environment**
- **increase your reading speed by eliminating poor reading habits**
- **match your reading speed to your reading material**
- **improve your comprehension of printed material**
- **find the information you need quickly**

A GOOD READING ENVIRONMENT IS UP TO YOU

It is difficult to read when you are tired, distracted, or uncomfortable. You can influence your reading rate and level of comprehension by setting up circumstances that make it easy to read. Here are some suggestions:

- *Read where you are comfortable, but not too comfortable.* For serious reading, an upright position is usually best. Slouching can actually be uncomfortable after a while; lying on the floor or

An upright position is best for reading. Lying on the floor or bed can make you sleepy.

bed can make you sleepy. If you will be making notes, sit at a desk or table.

- *Eliminate distracting sounds.* Voices from the nearby television and conversations are bound to interfere with your concentration, but music can actually mask other distracting sounds. Keep the volume down, and select something familiar to listen to that will not grab your attention.
- *Use good lighting to avoid eyestrain.* Natural light is best whenever possible; after dark, use incandescent lighting. If your eyes tire easily, are often red or sting, or if you have frequent headaches while reading, see a doctor—you may be helped by glasses.

BAD HABITS SLOW YOU DOWN

Most people don't recall very much about learning to read. However, certain habits formed in the early stages of learning to read may remain and slow your reading. These habits are inefficient; eliminating them will increase your reading speed.

- *Mouthing the words.* This "look-say" habit will really slow you down. Don't say the words aloud as you read. Always read silently and don't move your lips. If you find yourself moving your lips, try chewing gum or keeping a finger on your lips while you read.
- *Saying the words to yourself.* Pronouncing each word in your mind also takes time. This word-by-word approach is a difficult habit to break. Good readers don't focus on each word: They take in chunks at a time.
- *Finger-reading.* Don't use your finger to point at the words; don't use a ruler or bookmark to follow the lines of print. If you have these habits, keep your hands in your lap.

- *Head-following.* Moving your head to follow the lines of print uses more time than you realize. Keep your head still—put your hands on each side of your face or rest your chin on your hand.
- *Rereading unnecessarily.* Going back to reread can become a habit. Make yourself concentrate so you get it the first time through. If lack of concentration is not the problem, simply read on—often the meaning will become clear.
- *Eye-wandering; staring.* Loss of concentration can also cause you to lose your place or stare fixedly at a word. These time wasters are often a result of some of the inefficient habits described above. The slower you read, the more likely you are to lose your concentration.

MATCHING YOUR READING RATE TO THE MATERIAL

The goal for increasing your reading rate is not simply to finish the material in less time. If you read too fast, you may miss important points and sacrifice comprehension. The goal is to read at a rate that is appropriate to the kind of material you are reading. You can speed through comic books and magazines, but you will need to take longer to read textbooks and scholarly essays.

You likely automatically adjust your reading rate to each reading task. But if you suspect that you read everything at the same rate, make a conscious effort to match speed with need. The following considerations will help you.

1. *The reason for reading.* Are you reading for pleasure or for information? *Pleasure reading,* reading for entertainment and relaxation, may be done rapidly. Examples are fast-paced novels and the celebrity magazine you read for distraction in the dentist's waiting room. There are different levels of *reading for information.* You read magazines and newspapers to keep generally informed. You read textbooks to learn new information, ideas, and concepts. In each case, you read to the level of detail and comprehension that is necessary for your purpose.
2. *The level of difficulty.* If the material is fairly easy and you need only to remember the most important facts, read as quickly as possible. If the material is complex—filled with difficult concepts and many important details—you will need to read slowly and carefully.
3. *Your familiarity with the subject matter.* Your background, experience, and prior knowledge are significant factors in determining the speed at which you can read a selection effectively. The more familiar you are with the subject matter, the more rapidly you will be able to read. If the material is new to you, *previewing* strategies (see below) can help increase your speed and comprehension.

IMPROVING YOUR COMPREHENSION

To read something new and difficult, you may need to read at half your usual rate. But reading slowly does not guarantee that you will understand the material. Textbook reading in particular requires that you do more. To be able to understand and later recall what you read, you must become an *active reader.*

Active readers think about what they are going to read. They consider what they already know about the subject. They think about what the reading selection might cover. They think of questions which they would like answered as a result of reading the selection. These *pre-reading* activities help readers set a purpose for reading the selection: to find the answers to questions.

"Questioning is the door of knowledge."
—Irish proverb

You may be wondering how to create questions about something you have not yet started to read. The active reader can do this by *previewing* the reading selection. Actually, you probably do this all the time without realizing it: You glance at a book's table of contents or look at pictures, captions, and headings as you flip through chapters. This gives you a sense of what the selection is about and may trigger questions that will guide your reading.

S Q 3 R (The "SQRCube"): READING STRATEGIES THAT WORK

The time and effort you spend on activities *before* you read will add greatly to your comprehension when you read the selection. In addition, there are activities you can do *after* reading that will strengthen your understanding and your ability to recall the information at a later time.

Many students have found success with a system of techniques developed by Francis Robinson in 1941. This system is known as *S Q 3 R*, which stands for **S**urvey, **Q**uestion, **R**ead, **R**ecite, **R**eview.

MEMORY TRICK: S Q 3 R

SURVEY the section for main ideas and general organization.
QUESTION to set a purpose and guide your reading.
READ the selection to find the answers to your questions.
RECITE your questions and answers at a later time.
REVIEW your questions and answers at a later time.

Take a closer look at each element of this effective approach to reading textbooks and nonfiction articles.

SURVEY

A survey, or preview, will acquaint you with the main ideas and organization of the reading assignment. When you survey, ***skim*** the entire selection by reading the following:

- the title
- all headings and subheadings
- the introduction or first paragraph
- the first sentence of each paragraph
- all words in special type (bold or italic)
- all graphics (pictures, charts, diagrams)
- the last paragraph or conclusion

Your aim in previewing is to pinpoint the main ideas. Skimming will not necessarily reveal the meaning of these ideas, but it will alert you to their importance. And when you read the selection, you will already be a little familiar with the main ideas. Studies have shown that even this limited familiarity can lead to a twofold increase in comprehension when you read the entire selection.

During the survey, you also become familiar with the way the piece is organized. You can see patterns in how the information is presented. Since the brain works well with patterns it has experienced, becoming familiar with the style and order of presentation will aid comprehension.

QUESTION

You will get more out of reading if you establish what you want or expect to learn before you begin to read. Here are some sources of questions.

- *Questions at the end of sections, chapters, and units.* Part of your survey should be to read these questions so that you will have them in mind when you read the selection.
- *Teacher-provided questions.* Pay attention to these even if a written answer is not required. Read them carefully and refer to them often as you read.
- *Questions suggested by headings.* During your survey, turn every heading into a question by asking ***who, what, where, when, why,*** or ***how.*** Other questions may follow, as in this example using a science text heading:

  Types of Bacteria

  Questions: ***What*** are the types of bacteria?
  How are they different?
  Where are they found?
- *Questions suggested by words in special print.* Key words and concepts are usually in bold or italic type. In the chapter on

bacteria, you might see *binary fission* or *Louis Pasteur;* in your geometry text, *isosceles* or *equilateral.*

Creating questions may help to reveal the general topic of the selection. If your questions are about the Oregon Trail, the Mexican War, and the Gold Rush, the topic is most likely Westward Expansion.

READ

Read each portion of the assignment with your questions in mind. They will alert you to the information in the selection. You have tuned your brain to receive the information, much the way you tune your radio to a favorite station.

As you are reading, continue to form questions: How does this information relate to the main topic? How does it relate to information I have just read? If you can see the framework connecting the ideas, you will be able to process the information more easily.

- *Mental images increase comprehension and memory*. Your comprehension will be greatly helped if you create *mental* pictures as you read. Visualizing people, events, and objects will be easy; it will take practice to visualize ideas and concepts. It will be worth the effort because it will not only increase comprehension, it will also strengthen your memory: Visual images are very powerful for most people.
- *Should you take notes as you read?* It can be very helpful to take notes as you read but *don't overdo it.* Write down the information that pertains to your questions and brief definitions of any new terms. Don't use complete sentences; use abbreviations and symbols to keep your notes short. If possible, make graphic organizers that show important relationships.

When you want more information, stop to consult references or other sources. Or, if you don't want to interrupt the

Studies show that students who recite can recall four times as much material two weeks later.

flow of your reading, make a note to explore further after you have finished the selection.

RECITE

After you have finished reading, recite the questions and answers aloud. You can do this alone or with a study partner. Many teachers feel students learn best by explaining to others what they know. And studies show that students who recite can recall four times as much material two weeks later. Students remember about 80 percent of the material if they recite immediately after reading, compared to only 20 percent if they do not.

If you did not take notes while you read, do so now. Repeating the information helps make it part of your long-term memory. And the act of writing is physical, involving muscle activity; studies show that combining thinking with movement plants knowledge even deeper in your memory.

"Men learn while they teach."

—Seneca, Roman philosopher

REVIEW

This final step is essential to ensure deep comprehension and good recall of the information at a later time. Review a few hours after you have finished reading and reciting or a few days later. Re-read the headings, review the answers to your questions; go over your notes. A good review takes only a short time; if you review periodically, the information will be easy to recall at test time.

"Repetition is the mother of learning."
—Russian proverb

When you review, you may find that something that was originally difficult or confusing makes perfect sense. You notice new things: how the ideas relate to the topic or how the topic relates to a previous one. Make additional notes on your findings.

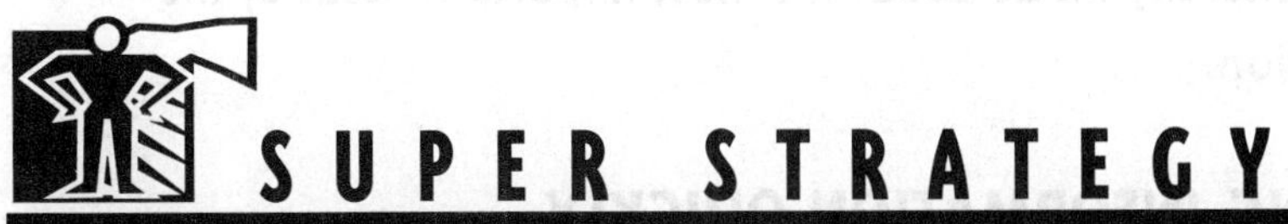

KEEPING ON TRACK

PREDICTING **is a way to monitor your comprehension as you read. Predict what is likely to happen; read to find out. If you were wrong, think about why. Then use what you know to predict what will happen next; read to evaluate that prediction. If you are wrong more than you are right, you need to improve your comprehension. Here are some "fix-up" strategies that can improve your general comprehension or increase your understanding of a difficult passage:**

- ***Slow down as the passage becomes harder.*** **Your goal should be to read as quickly as you can and still understand the ideas.**

Don't be in a rush to finish.

- ***Reread if necessary.*** **Read a sentence again; re-read the previous sentence or two.**
- ***Move ahead.*** **Sometimes you can clarify something by simply reading a bit further. A complex sentence may become clear when you read the next one.**
- ***Use the resources at hand.*** **Look in the glossary in the back of the book, in the dictionary, in an encyclopedia. A little more information may be all it takes to clear up your confusion.**
- ***Consult a simpler resource.*** **There are times when you may have to read lower-level material first. This will give you the background you need to understand your difficult assignment.**
- ***Use your experience.*** **You will gain in meaning and comprehension when you relate to the material on a personal level. The stronger the personal links, the more you will remember later.**
- ***Watch for "signal" words.*** **Words such as *therefore, because, since, thus,* and *consequently* indicate a conclusion. Conclusions are generally made about the most important ideas of the selection.**

FINDING INFORMATION QUICKLY

Sometimes you need to find specific information quickly. In that case, you may need to read only parts of a selection. ***Scan*** the selection until you find the information. When scanning, do not read every word: Let your eyes glide over the selection. Glance at each paragraph, but don't read unless it contains something about the information you seek. When you have the information you need, stop scanning.

This selective reading technique saves time when used appropriately to gather specific information. It should not be used in place of deep reading when you need to understand concepts.

For a preview or overview, skimming the entire selection would be appropriate. The Thumbs Up section in this chapter will help you see when scanning would be useful; The Thumbs Down section tells when it would not be appropriate.

SCANNING

THUMBS UP; do scan

- an encyclopedia article to find out when Thomas Jefferson died
- a pie graph in your social studies text to find out what percentage of New Yorkers earn under $20,000
- your algebra notes to find out how to simplify radicals
- the bio chapter on mammals for a definition of *marsupial*
- the subject file of the library's computer database for books on aeronautics
- the chapter you read previously for a detail you wish to include in an essay you are writing

THUMBS DOWN; don't scan

- when you need to find an article in support of gun control (instead *skim* several articles to get an idea of the author's opinion)
- when you need to understand a complex issue (*deep read* several sources)
- when you need to select books for your research project (*skim* the table of contents, index, and chapter titles to determine if the book will be useful)
- when you want to get a general impression of an article in *American Heritage* (*skim* to see what information it covers)
- when you are asked to evaluate a reasoned argument presented in an essay (*deep read* to be able to follow the line of reasoning, make inferences, and uncover logic fallacies)

SUPER TACTIC

USING SQ3R IN SOCIAL STUDIES

Social studies—history, government, geography, and sociology—explore how people function and relate in a society or community. In many cases, these relationships are often a matter of interpretation. The way one sees the rights and duties of citizens, for example, depends on factors such as one's background and upbringing.

Since one historian or sociologist may view a subject differently from another, critical thinking is essential when reading in social studies. The S Q 3 R system will help you analyze and evaluate the information you read. Below are some special considerations that apply to social studies.

- **SURVEY**

  In addition to previewing the content of a reading selection, you should strive to uncover the author's viewpoint. Read the information about the author's background that may accompany the selection. Skim the selection for clues to the author's opinion. This will help you judge the validity of the source before you begin to read.

- **EVALUATE PRIMARY AS WELL AS SECONDARY SOURCES**

  A *primary source* is information reported by someone who was present at the time of an event, or a document, map, photograph, or object produced at that time. For example, a 1960 newspaper article about the election of John F. Kennedy is a primary source of information. A *secondary* source is information reported by someone who did not experience the event. A history of the Renaissance, written in 1997, is a secondary source. So is your social studies textbook.

  Historians and other researchers use primary sources whenever they can. Historian Edith Hamilton, in the preface to her book, *The*

Roman Way, says that "the writings of the day show the quality of the people as no historical reconstruction can." Although this is true, and you should consult primary sources when possible, remember to read and judge them critically since they are shaped by the author's point of view.

> "What his imagination is to the poet, facts are to the historian. His exercise of judgment comes in their selection, his art in their arrangement."
>
> —Barbara Tuchman, historian

- QUESTION

Most questions for a social studies selection will come from the usual sources: headings, key terms, end of chapter, teacher suggestion. If you are studying a period of history chronologically, the class lecture or your knowledge of the historical period may prompt some questions for the next reading.

Because history is so event-oriented, it easily lends itself to *who, what, where,* and *when* questions. But don't stop there: Be sure to also ask why something happened and how it affected something else. Otherwise, you'll end up with unrelated bits of information. *How* and *why* questions will help reveal the theme; when you read, you'll be ready to connect information to that theme for greater understanding.

- READ

As you read, you will be tempted to concentrate on people, places, dates, and events. You assume that your teacher will expect you to learn these historical facts, so why not start now? Resist the temptation. Refer to your thoughtful questions about *how* these facts are related; read to fully understand these connections.

Taking notes while you read can keep you alert and help focus your concentration. You may find it easy to outline from your social studies book since most texts are organized in outline format. Concentrate on the main ideas and the details that support the main ideas to build your comprehension.

Visualizing also increases your comprehension. Mentally picture what you are reading. Make sketches, charts, and diagrams. If appropriate, create a time line to help you keep track of important events. Examine events that happened about the same time; think how these events may have affected each other.

Stop to consult references or other sources for more information when necessary. But this may push you off the track. Certainly stop if you cannot understand enough to go on; otherwise, place a self-stick note at a passage you would like to explore further when you are finished reading.

- RECITE

Since there are many facts you will have to recall at a later time, be sure to recite your questions and answers immediately after you finish the selection. Remember that movement embeds knowledge deep in your memory. Try acting out your answers when possible.

- REVIEW

A good way to review is to write a brief summary of the selection in your own words. Your summary of a short article should be only a sentence or two; of a long article or textbook chapter, a paragraph or two. The summary should include not only what the selection states but also anything it implies. Reading articles often requires you to think critically: Make inferences, note similarities and differences, relate cause and effect. A summary is your *interpretation* of the information in the selection.

FOR REVIEW

1. What makes a good reading environment?
2. What are six reading habits that slow you down?
3. What are the three considerations that determine how fast you should try to read ?
4. How does previewing help your concentration?
5. List some sources of prereading questions.
6. Why should you visualize as you read?
7. How does predicting keep you on track?
8. Why is it important to determine an author's point of view?

AT-A-GLANCE SOCIAL STUDIES SECTION

GEOGRAPHY

Continents		The Oceans from largest to smallest
Africa	**Eastern Hemisphere**	Pacific Ocean
Antarctica	Africa	Atlantic Ocean
Asia	Asia	Indian Ocean
Australia	Australia	Arctic Ocean
Europe	Europe	
North America		
South America		
	Western Hemisphere	
	North America	
	South America	

latitude (east-west lines): distance north or south of the equator
longitude (north-south lines): distance east or west of the prime meridian
Equator: line of 0° latitude (equidistant from North and South Poles)
prime meridian: line of 0° longitude (runs through Greenwich, England)
North Pole: located at 90° North latitude
South Pole: located at 90° South latitude

ECOLOGY

acid rain: rain or snow that has picked up a high concentration of acid by falling through air pollution

biome: one of Earth's major ecological communities—forest (including rain forests), grassland, tundra, desert

biosphere: the parts of Earth where life exists, from the bottom of the sea to the lower atmosphere

drought: a long period without rain

ecosystem: living and nonliving things functioning as a unit in their environment; may be aquatic or terrestrial

erosion: the movement of weathered material from one place to another; agents are water, ice, and wind

global warming: the rising temperature of Earth caused by the trapping of heat under a blanket of carbon dioxide and other gases in the atmosphere (the greenhouse effect)

U.S. GOVERNMENT

LEGISLATIVE BRANCH:

Congress (Senate and House of Representatives)

Congress makes the laws, which must pass by a majority vote of both the Senate and the House.

Checks and balances: The president can veto a bill; Congress can override this veto by a two-thirds vote of the entire Congress. The Senate can refuse to appoint a cabinet member or a judge or to approve the budget. See ***impeachment.***

JUDICIAL BRANCH:

The Supreme Court of the United States

The part of government that judges whether laws passed by Congress and actions of the president are in agreement with the Constitution. Federal court judges, including the Supreme Court Justices, are appointed by the president for life.

Checks and balances: A judicial ruling that a law or presidential action is *unconstitutional* carries the force of law. The Senate checks the judicial branch by approving or denying appointments.

EXECUTIVE BRANCH:

President, Vice President, Cabinet

This branch sees that the laws made by Congress are carried out. The president is chosen by the *electoral college* after a popular election.

Checks and balances: The president has veto power over bills proposed by Congress; the president's selection of his Cabinet and certain other officials needs the approval of the Senate.

IMPEACHMENT

The House of Representatives may accuse, or *impeach,* the president and certain other government officials for high crimes, such as treason or bribery. The trial is held in the Senate; two-thirds of the Senate must vote to convict. If convicted, the president or other official must leave office and may never hold a federal office again. No president has been convicted by the Senate, though Andrew Johnson was *impeached,* or officially accused, in 1868. Richard Nixon resigned the presidency in 1974 before he could be tried on impeachment charges in the Senate.

6 TEST TAKING

Tests serve many purposes. They help you and your teacher measure your mastery of a subject. A test can tell you what you know and what you don't know. The mistakes you make on a test can indicate where you need help if you are to improve. And tests give you the opportunity to show that you *have* improved.

For all these reasons, tests are an important part of academic life. The more you know about test-taking strategies, the more confident and successful you will be.

THIS CHAPTER WILL SHOW YOU

- **how to reduce test anxiety**
- **the most effective studying methods**
- **simple memory devices**
- **general test-taking strategies**
- **strategies for objective tests**
- **when and how to guess**
- **how to handle essay tests**
- **how to do your best on standardized tests**

TEST ANXIETY

How you feel about taking a test can have a direct effect on how well you do. It is normal to have butterflies in your stomach; a little anxiety can actually keep you alert. But too much anxiety can cause you to become ill or freeze when you must be ready to perform.

One crucial way to lessen anxiety is to plan ahead. At the beginning of the semester, ask your teacher for a test schedule. If the test dates aren't available, perhaps the teacher can supply you with a general idea of when tests will occur: after every chapter, after each unit, at midterm and end term, for example.

"To be prepared is to have no anxiety."
—Korean proverb

During the term, pace yourself. Finish all projects and papers on time. Set an earlier deadline for yourself if you see that a project will be due near a test; you need several days to prepare for a test. Allowing enough time to adequately prepare will greatly reduce anxiety.

There are techniques for reducing anxiety when the time of the test is close. Their effectiveness varies from person to person and with practice; the more experience you have with a technique, the greater its effect at test time.

1. *Exercise.* Exercise reduces nervous energy and increases mental alertness. Try mild exercise—a walk or a few calisthenics—before or during study or when tension builds up prior to the test. However, exercise right before bedtime may make it diffi-

Exercise reduces nervous energy and increases mental alertness.

cult for you to fall asleep: If you feel anxious the night before a test, try one of the other methods of relaxation.

2. *Meditation.* The goal of meditation is to empty your mind of all thoughts. This is sometimes accomplished by repeating a mantra, or special phrase, over and over, but there are other ways to block out thoughts. Some people focus on something in the room; others close their eyes and imagine a peaceful scene.
3. *Deep breathing.* Slow deep breathing is especially good for dispelling moments of anxiety before they become acute. Take a deep slow breath, exhale; take several regular breaths; if necessary, take another deep slow breath. Make sure to do enough regular breathing in between: Too much deep breathing can cause you to hyperventilate and become dizzy and lightheaded.
4. *Positive thinking.* If anxiety distracts you as you study for a test, remind yourself how much more you know than when you began to review. If anxiety strikes during the test, tell yourself that you're prepared and that you've survived other tests. Of

course, a positive attitude cannot alone overcome unrealistic expectations: You must couple it with solid preparation.

EFFECTIVE STUDY METHODS

Your studying can be more effective if you know what the test format will be.

The items on an objective test require you to recall facts: When you study, concentrate on remembering details. If you are expecting an essay test, concentrate more on patterns and relationships: similarities, differences, and cause and effect. Sometimes tests are a combination of types. Most teachers will tell you what to expect.

"Memory is like a purse—if it be over-full that it cannot shut, all will drop out of it."

—Thomas Fuller,
17th-century English author

Avoid cramming. After a few hours your studying becomes much less effective. Experts have found that you learn best when study sessions are spread over several days. On the first day, think about what might be on the test. A brief review will remind you of the main ideas and concepts you have covered. Skim the following:

- the chapter summary
- previous quizzes, classwork, and homework
- questions you created to guide your reading (see Chapter Five)
- notes from lectures and the textbook

On the next day, review in detail. Read and highlight your notes; write key words in the margins. Make note cards for formulas you need to memorize. Recite these aloud; recite the questions and answers you created. Writing and reciting help store this information in your long-term memory. Other techniques to improve memory are in a separate section later in this chapter.

The third day can be a combination of review and self-quizzing. Review your highlighted notes and the key words in the margins. Then cover your notes and try to recite the information that goes with each key word. Also cover and recite the answers to the questions you created. Write out formulas and check these against your note cards. Make additional note cards of any information you still have trouble recalling—put the question or key word on the front and the answer on the back. Quiz yourself until you have mastered the material.

On your last day of studying, make up a test for yourself. Include some new questions—you know more now! Put the questions in the form you expect for the actual test—essay, objective, or a combination. Think about the class lectures: If facts were stressed, create factual questions; if concepts were stressed, create essay questions about those concepts.

One very effective strategy when you're studying for an essay test is to make up six essay questions based on major topics covered in class. Then write an outline for your response to each. Be thorough; if you feel you are missing important information, give yourself time to remember it. Then compare what you included with information in your notes and in the text. Save these outlines for a final review at the end of the study session. Finally, choose one of the questions for a full response. Allow yourself no more than 20 minutes to cover the major points and include at least two details about each. With the time limit, your writing may not be polished, but your reasoning and supporting statements should be strong and complete. You may have even less time on the test.

IMPROVING YOUR MEMORY

Some people are blessed with excellent memories, but most need help in remembering information. You can use the study strategies discussed earlier to help you memorize: reciting aloud, using visual images, and timing sessions carefully. Here are some guidelines for applying these strategies to memorization.

- Reciting with a study partner can have an added benefit at test time: The partner's voice may come to you when your memory fails. Also try to combine reciting with a physical activity, such as writing margin notes.
- Writing notes and key words also involves visual images, another boost to strengthening memory. Draw diagrams of the information; later, close your eyes and visualize them.
- Spreading study over several days helps long-term memory. Sleep *at least* six hours after a session to imprint the memory in your brain. Sessions that concentrate on memorization should last no longer than two hours, and you should take frequent *short* breaks. Finally, sessions should not be too far apart; try not to miss a day.

You can also improve your memory by making an association between what you want to remember and something else. For example, to remember that the capital of **Kansas** is **To**peka, think of this line from *The Wizard of Oz:*

> "**To**to, I have a feeling we're not in **Kansas** anymore."

The association works as a hook to pull in the information you need If you've never seen *The Wizard of Oz,* create an association that works for you.

MEMORY TRICK: RITA

Let RITA help you remember:

RECITE aloud until you can do it from memory.
IMAGES deepen your memory.
TIME between sessions is necessary for long-term memory.
ASSOCIATE what you need to know with something meaningful to you.

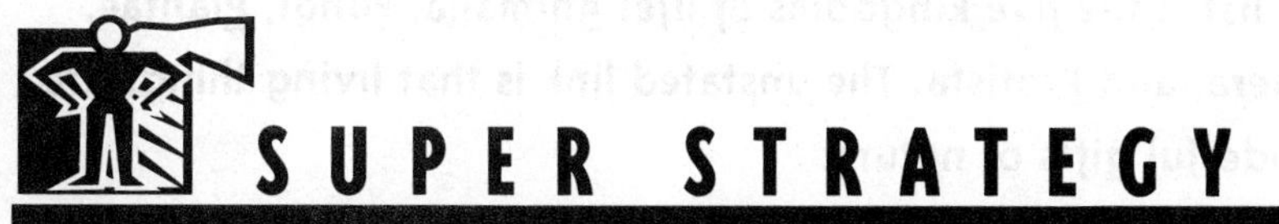

SUPER STRATEGY

MEMORY DEVICES

The memory hooks below are called *mnemonic devices.* They are particularly helpful for remembering lists of items. There are three basic types of mnemonic devices.

- *Word cues.* Create a word from the first letter of each item of a list you need to remember. For example, to remember the Great Lakes, think of HOMES (Huron, Ontario, Michigan, Erie, Superior). You will find it even easier to remember if you add a visual association: picture lake-front HOMES.
- *Nonsense names.* Create a name from the initial letters of words in a list. Many people remember the range of colors in a spectrum by associating it with Roy G. Biv (red, orange, yellow, green, blue, indigo, and violet).
- *Phrases or sentences.* Create a sentence using the initial letters of the words in the list for the initial letters of the words in your sentence. This works well when the list is too long to create a

word or name. Learn the order of the planets with this sentence:

My very educated mother just showed us nine planets. It stands for:

Mercury, Venus, Earth, Mars, Jupiter, Saturn, Uranus, Neptune, Pluto.

The sentence cues the two M planets: My and Mercury end in y, and mother and Mars (almost) end in r. It even includes the topic: nine planets. It is not necessary to include the topic, but do so if you are afraid your memory needs help linking the sentence to its topic.

In some cases, the link to the topic is personal but unstated. This list is the five kingdoms of life: Animalia, Fungi, Plantae, Monera, and Protista. The unstated link is that living things are wonderful gifts of nature:

A present for me, please. (Note the pr and pl cues)

Since the order of items in the list is not important, many different sentences could be made; here is another:

Pro football players attack monuments.

This suggests players attacking granite statues at blocking practice. The silliness of the image may stick in your mind; the *mon* in *monument* will help you remember the unfamiliar Monera. The silliness doesn't matter as long as the association helps you remember. That's the secret of using memory devices.

GENERAL TEST-TAKING STRATEGIES

Once you've done everything to prepare for the test, it's time to relax. Allow yourself some free time before bed. Listen to music or do a little light reading. Be sure to get a good night's sleep and don't forget to set your alarm: Tomorrow is TEST DAY!

TEST TAKING

THUMBS UP

- Check that you have all needed supplies—pencils, erasers, watch, possibly a calculator (including extra batteries).
- Arrive at the test early; select a good seat where you will be comfortable and not be distracted.
- Listen carefully to all spoken instructions; read all written directions.
- Look over the entire test before you begin to answer any questions.
- Plan how much time to devote to each question according to point values; stick to this "time budget."
- Answer the easy questions first; mark the ones you skip and go back to them later.
- Review the questions and your answers if you finish before time is up.

THUMBS DOWN

- Sleep to the last possible moment and skip breakfast.
- Fail to keep in mind all test directions. (Why answer every question if only three out of five are required?)
- Read the questions carelessly. Every word is important; underline key words, such as not or always.
- Read more into a question than is really there or make your answer more involved than it needs to be.
- Select the first answer that seems right. (Consider all possible answers.)
- Write sloppily to save time. (Your answer may be illegible or misinterpreted.)
- Panic when others begin handing in their tests. (Work at your own pace and use all of the time available to recheck your test.)

STRATEGIES FOR TAKING OBJECTIVE TESTS

Objective tests are those requiring the recall of information. They tend to concentrate on facts but may test your understanding of concepts as well. Objective tests may include true-false, matching,

True-false statements demand very careful reading.

multiple-choice, and completion items, or a combination of these.

Objective tests present opportunities for guessing. In most teacher-created tests, your score is based *only* on your correct answers. In this situation, by all means guess—an unfilled blank earns no credit. If you guess correctly, you will earn points; an incorrect guess has no penalty. In some cases (often with standardized tests) there is a "guessing penalty"—the score you earn with correct answers will be *reduced* by wrong answers. This makes the decision to guess a little more difficult. Most experts agree that you should not make wild guesses. In each section below, there are suggestions that may increase your chances of guessing correctly.

TRUE-FALSE STATEMENTS

True-false statements demand very careful reading. Certain types of words should put you on alert. Words such as *all, always, only, none, never, no one,* and *everyone* often make a statement false. For example, you learned that cirrus clouds usually indicate fair weather. On a test, you read the following:

Cirrus clouds always signal fair weather ahead.

The qualifying *always* makes the statement *false,* since cirrus clouds aren't a fair weather predictor absolutely every time they occur.

There are other qualifying words that more often make a statement true: *frequently, often, probably, rarely, usually, generally, sometimes,* and *many* are common examples.

When a statement has more than one part, *every* part must be considered. Be wary of combination statements; check each part, and mark it true only if each part is true. Here is an example of a combination statement:

Cumulo-nimbus and strato-cumulus clouds often produce rain.

Although the first type of cloud often produces an afternoon thunderstorm, the second *rarely* produces rain. Since not *all* parts are true, mark this statement *false.* In fact, the longer a statement is, the more suspicious you should be; if forced to guess, mark complex, multi-part statements false.

Once you have read a statement very carefully and have made your decision, you should usually stay with that decision. Change your answer only if you become convinced you have misread or misunderstood the statement or that you have made a factual mistake.

MATCHING ITEMS

Objective tests sometimes include a section requiring you to match items in two columns. Usually one column has short entries—often just terms; the other column of longer entries gives details or descriptions of the terms. Since the terms are often closely related, you must take care to make the *best* possible match. Here is how to proceed.

1. Begin by reading both columns to become familiar with all possibilities. Underline key words.
2. Then carefully examine the first item in the column of *longer* entries.
3. Scan the entire column of short entries for a proper match. If you are *sure* you have the best one, indicate the match according to the test directions. Cross out the items you have used.
4. If you're *not* sure, skip that long entry: If you guess, you eliminate the term you select as a possibility for any other match. Put a check beside the entry so you remember to return to it later.
5. Go to the next long entry. Scan the remaining choices—remember to cross out the term you select or put a check beside an entry that you skip.
6. When you have made all the matches you are sure of, look for relationship clues among the ones that remain. If a term in one column is somehow associated with a word in another, it may be a good match.

MULTIPLE CHOICE

Read multiple choice questions carefully; watch for qualifying words.

> "Which formula will *always* work to find...."
> "All of the following are correct *except*.... "

And then you must read *all* the choices because often they are quite similar; one may seem OK, but another might be *better.* There also may be possibilities such as *all of the above* or *none of the above* or *a and b, a and e,* etc.

Once you have read the question and all of its answers carefully, cross out any choices that are obviously incorrect. Then select the choice that best answers the question. Check that the completed statement reads smoothly—your answer should "sound right," and the grammar should be consistent for the entire statement.

If you are unsure of the answer but can eliminate two of the choices, make an educated guess based on knowledge of the question, or consider these tips.

- Choose the longer of the two remaining answers.
- Don't make a choice based on frequency; the fact that you haven't selected c for a while doesn't make it a good choice.
- The first answer is statistically the *least* likely to be correct, especially on a teacher-created test.
- "All of the above" is a good choice if at least two are correct and the others are not obviously wrong.

Remember, if there is no penalty for guessing, choose *something*; a blank will always be wrong.

"Guess, if you can, and choose, if you dare."
—Corneille, 17th-century French dramatist

COMPLETIONS

These test items are sentences that require completion. Some have more than one blank; make sure you fill in each. Often the test item comes directly from the text or from a class lecture. Read the item carefully at first; if you don't know the answer, reread the item a few times. If the item is based on a familiar statement, repetition may help the missing piece pop into your mind.

There are often context clues in the items, particularly in the longer ones.

Also notice the grammar of the sentence; this can help you figure out an answer. For example, a sentence on your Civil War test reads

Frederick Douglass was an ____________________.

The *an* is a clue that the answer starts with a vowel: *abolitionist.*

Never assume the length of the blank is an indicator of the length of the answer. The number of blanks, however, can be a helpful clue. If there are four blanks in a row separated by commas, the answer you are looking for may be a list of four items. Perhaps you have memorized such a list related to the question's topic. Try it out—see if it makes sense when you plug your list into the blanks.

Since most completions are looking for an exact word or words, guessing can be difficult. If there is not a penalty and you have *any* idea for an answer related to the item's topic, make a guess. It's possible that you are correct, or you may receive partial credit for being generally "on the subject." However you fill in each blank, be sure to test your answer: Does it fit the item logically, structurally, and grammatically? As in multiple choice items, the completed sentence should read smoothly and should make sense.

HOW TO HANDLE ESSAY QUESTIONS

If taking a combination test, always do the objective sections first. Those items often contain details that you can include in an essay. Read the directions for the essay section carefully—don't write three essays if only two are required. Then read each question carefully. Underline key words and notice test terminology: The word *describe* does not tell you to do the same thing as does the word *justify*. The Reference section at the end of this chapter contains a list of test terminology.

Budget your time carefully when answering essay questions.

Keeping your time budget in mind, outline your response. If time is very short, list or map your major points and supporting details. An essay usually follows this format:

- *Introductory paragraph.* Turn the question's words into a statement of your position, or thesis, in the first sentence. Then briefly summarize the major points you will make in support of your thesis; three major points are usual in a test essay.
- *Body of three paragraphs.* Discuss each major point in a separate paragraph. State the point in the first sentence, then give details and examples to support that point. Be clear and concise: Make sure your reasoning is logical and stick to the point being developed. Use words such as *consequently* and *in support of* to indicate connections you are making. See the Reference section for other "indicator" words.
- *Concluding paragraph.* Restate your thesis in this paragraph and tie the main points together. You may include a *very brief* summary of these points and the evidence you gave to support them. You should not include anything new.

Your writing may not be as polished as you'd like, but test essays are generally graded more on substance than on style: Your

teacher will be looking for content and organization. It helps to leave a line or two between papagraphs for neat revisions. If you are using a blue book, consider writing only on the right-hand page—leave the left-hand page for revisions.

If you run out of time, copy down the remainder of your outline as completely as possible and write *Out of time*. A well-developed outline that shows your grasp of the material may earn you partial credit. If time is not the problem—you have difficulty answering the essay question—think about *anything* related to the topic. Relax and let your mind roam broadly—perhaps you can come close enough to the topic to craft an essay worth some credit. Just be sure your essay is focused and well-developed.

TAKING STANDARDIZED TESTS

Your performance on standardized tests, such as the Iowa Test and the Scholastic Aptitude Test (SAT), will be enhanced by the consistent use of the effective test-taking strategies already discussed. This section offers additional recommendations for tactically applying these strategies to standardized tests.

Standardized tests usually consist of questions that test your math and verbal skills in a multiple-choice format. Answers are entered in grids on a separate sheet. Although the tests are designed to measure ability more than the recall of factual information, there is much that you can do to prepare.

Knowing what to expect will help you spend your preparation time wisely. Talk to students who have taken the particular test.

They may give you some general pointers and offer some assurance as well. Ask your English and math teachers for advice. They may pinpoint specific areas in which you need improvement.

Go to the school library, public library, or bookstore for a book or CD-ROM software review program about your specific test. These review books and software programs include what the test covers, the format, and sample tests. Look for books that include actual timed practice tests; familiarity with test procedures and materials is invaluable. If you find a book or software program that you really like, consider buying it; you can write notes in it and use the answer grid that is usually provided or take practice tests on your home computer.

There are also review courses, most notably for the SAT. These courses review math and verbal skills and provide information on format, shortcuts, and guessing strategies. Most provide practice under actual testing conditions. Some high schools offer review courses or at least "word power" courses to improve vocabulary.

Make a conscious decision to put sufficient time and effort into your review. Whether you are taking a course or working on your own, begin at least two months before the test. Note any particular problems you have; concentrate on those areas. Learn new vocabulary words and practice analogies. If you find you are deficient in math, consider tutoring.

Good preparation should bring steady improvement—and a lessening of anxiety. Before test day, make sure you have all your supplies, especially a calculator (and extra batteries) if recommended, and any required admission forms. If the test is being held at a location that is new to you, make sure you know how to get there; a trial trip to the test site can be reassuring.

On test day, eat a good breakfast; the test may be quite long. If snacks are allowed, plan to bring one. Arrive as early as possible:

Find the testing room, choose your seat, arrange your supplies, and set your watch to the proper time. Be ready to listen to any spoken instructions; do *not* assume you know what to do.

When you receive your test, read all directions thoroughly. Familiarize yourself with the answer sheet. Note how much time is allotted to each section and plan accordingly; write down the "finish" time. Work steadily and without panic—many students cannot finish all parts of the test. Perhaps these special tips will help you:

- Answer the questions that you know first; mark those you skip in the test booklet, *not on the answer sheet.*
- Don't lose your place on the answer sheet; be especially careful when you skip a question.

- Read *all* choices before you make a response. Be alert for possibilities such as *none of the above, all of the above, no change,* and *II and III only.*
- If you are working with a critical reading passage, read its questions first; keep them in mind as you read the passage. Read the questions again before you choose an answer.
- Don't become bogged down on any one question. Mark it as a "skip" and move on; return later if there's time. One exception: when the questions relate to a passage you have read, don't plan to come back later—you may not remember the passage.
- Guessing can be a good option—at times. The penalty for guessing wrong is usually only a fraction of a point. If you can eliminate two obviously wrong answers out of five possibilities, certainly guess. Many students guess if they can eliminate at least one *and* the question is from their "strong" area. Do not guess if you can't eliminate more than one answer.
- Check and double-check that you are recording your answers in the right place each time you begin a new section; sometimes the answer sheet has spaces for more answers than there are questions.

- If you have time when you finish, look over your test. See if your answers make sense. For math, try a different method to see if you get the same result. Check that you do not have extra marks anywhere on your answer sheet.

Even if you do not finish the test, try not to worry. You may score well anyway. And remember, as important as the test may seem, it is not the only method that will ever be used to evaluate you. Continue to improve your abilities by studying hard and doing your best in school. In time, your efforts will earn you success.

FOR REVIEW

1. What are three ways to reduce test anxiety?
2. How can you apply three effective study techniques to memorization?
3. What is an example of a word cue or nonsense name association?
4. What does <u>RITA</u> stand for?
5. How would you set a time budget for a test?
6. What questions should you answer first on a test? Why?
7. What are two qualifying words that usually make a statement false?
8. What is the format of a test essay?

TEST TERMINOLOGY

Term used	Your response should include:
name, list	a list of the items requested (no details)
define	the meaning; the class it is part of
describe	details and examples that show what it is; summarize the main points
outline	the main points and their supporting details
illustrate	examples to clarify a point
trace	how it developed; usually chronologically
explain	how or why something happened
compare	similarities and differences
contrast	differences only
distinguish	how it differs from others that are similar
discuss	all points of view; pros and cons
criticize	your opinion—provide reasons, pros and cons
interpret	an explanation in terms of your own knowledge
evaluate	your judgment of its advantages and disadvantages
defend	details that prove it or prove its worth
prove	evidence or logical reasons to establish it is true

INDICATOR WORDS

These words will alert the reader of your essay that you are about to provide significant information, show a relationship, or draw a conclusion.

also	*moreover*
consequently	*nevertheless*
finally	*next*
first	*of course*
furthermore	*on the other hand*
however	*since*
in addition	*therefore*
in conclusion	*thus*

VOCABULARY-BUILDING ROOTS

alt—high (**alt**itude)
andro—man (**andro**gen)
anim—breath, spirit (in**anim**ate)
aud—hear (**aud**ition)
auto—self (**auto**nomous)
baro—weight (**baro**meter)
batho—depth (**batho**sphere)
belli—war (**belli**gerent)
ben, bene—good, well (**bene**ficent)
bio—life (**bio**genesis)
cap—head (re**cap**itulate)
cede, cess—go, yield (in**cess**antly)
chron—time (ana**chron**ism)
circum—around, about (**circum**scribe)
corp—body (**corp**oreal)
dem—people (epi**dem**ic)
dic, dict—speak (pre**dict**)
diplo—double (**diplo**matic)
edi—building (**edi**fication)
ethno—nation (**ethno**graphy)
fid—trust, faith (con**fid**ence)
fin—end, limit (de**fin**itive)
frac, frag—break (re**frac**tion)
gram, graph—writing (biblio**graph**y)
grat—pleasing (**grat**uitous)
grav—heavy (ag**grav**ate)
heli, helio—sun (**heli**um)
hora—season, time (**hora**ry)
hydr(o)—water (de**hydr**ate)
jud—judge (pre**jud**ice)
juv—young (re**juv**enate)
kine—motion (**kine**tic)
lat—side (col**lat**eral)
loc—place (**loc**alize)
luc, lum—light (il**lum**inate)
manu—hand (**manu**script)
medi—middle (**medi**ate)

mega, magn—great (**magn**animous)
neo, nov—new (**nov**itiate)
oper—work (in**oper**able)
ortho—straight (**ortho**dox)
pac—peace (**pac**ific)
palp—feel (**palp**able)
pec—money (im**pec**unious)
ped, pod—foot (arthro**pod**)
phos, photo—light (**phos**phorescent)
radi—root (**radi**cal)
rect—straight (cor**rect**)
rog—ask (inter**rog**ative)
rupt—break (ab**rupt**)
sema—sign (**sema**ntic)
sol—sun (**sol**stice)
sol—alone (**sol**ipsism)
soma—body (**soma**tic)
spec—look (retro**spec**tive)
somn—sleep (in**somn**ia)
tele—afar (**tele**pathy)
therm—heat (**therm**otactic)
topo—place (**topo**graphy)
urb—city (**urb**ane)
vac—empty (**vac**uous)
ven—come (con**ven**tion)
vita—life (**vita**lity)
vor—eat (carni**vor**ous)

7 LISTENING— AN OVERLOOKED SKILL

In school you learn how to write reports; you are taught to do complicated equations; you may even master a foreign language. Each of these skills depends, to some degree, on the ability to listen effectively. Listening is a primary method of acquiring much of the new information you absorb every day. It's how you sift the important material from the unimportant so you don't become overwhelmed by data. It's an essential tool in interacting with other people at school, at home, or at a part-time job. Yet, most people never take a listening course.

In this chapter, you'll have the opportunity to take a minicourse in listening.

IN THIS CHAPTER YOU WILL LEARN ABOUT:

- **various types of listening situations**
- **the skill of listening for patterns in classroom presentations**
- **listening more effectively to conversations**
- **looking for signal words in speech**
- **tuning into body language and voice inflection**
- **using listening skills on a part-time job**

LISTENING SITUATIONS

Communication involves at least two people: a sender and a receiver. Sometimes they communicate with each other through the printed word. For example, you might send someone a letter through the mail or a message over the Internet via E-mail. However, far more of the communicating you are likely to do will be oral. This means that you're speaking and listening. Indeed, experts say that people spend far more time engaged in listening than in any other form of communication.

An estimated 45 percent of our communication consists of listening. That's six times higher than the amount of writing we do and equal to the combined amount of talking and reading.

Listening occurs in a variety of situations:

- *Long distance.* Technology has enabled you to carry on a great deal of "distance listening" to a speaker who is not physically present. For example, you routinely listen to talk shows on television beamed to you by satellite from studios that may be thousands of miles away. Or you turn on the radio to get the latest weather report from a forecaster who is speaking from a station in another town. If you've ever been in a train station or an airport, you may have heard announcements over the loud speaker. These are one-way communications—you're not expected to say anything in response to them; we just listen. Telephone conversations are different, however. You speak as well as listen. And what you hear usually affects what you say in response.
- *Face-to-face dialogue.* Much of your listening occurs in short

Telephone conversations differ from other examples of distance listening because you speak as well as listen.

range conversations—one-on-one with a single individual, with several people, or in a large group. This morning, for instance, you may have heard your mother tell you that she had to work late today, so you'd have to prepare dinner. Last Saturday, you might have gone to a party and traded the latest gossip with a group of friends. Or yesterday afternoon you might have received some good advice from a co-worker at your after-school job that will make your work much easier. In all these conversations, there may have been a great deal of give and take, or you may have said very little. Nevertheless, listening plays a key role in each situation.

- *Formal situations.* As a student, you're usually required to spend a great deal of time listening in formal situations. In social studies or English class, for example, you're expected to pay attention as the teacher delivers lectures. And in science class, you're supposed to listen carefully as the teacher puts on complex demonstrations. Perhaps you belong to a sports team and receive frequent pep talks from your coach. If you've ever

As students, we're usually required to spend a great deal of our time listening in formal situations. So knowing how to listen can help you get the most out of each situation.

toured an art museum, you probably listened to a guide describe the paintings. In those situations, all the information generally flows in one direction. You're usually doing most of the listening while someone else is doing most of the talking. So knowing how to listen can help you get the most out of every situation.

SELECTIVE LISTENING

Every day, there is so much information coming your way that you can't possibly listen to all of it. Some, quite simply, goes in one ear and out the other. You may hear the words, but you don't analyze what they mean or store the information in your brain. Real listening involves adding value to what you hear—connecting what you hear with other thoughts and ideas, incorporating what you hear into your storehouse of knowledge to use later in solving problems and in making decisions. The fact is, people tend to listen selectively—that is, we absorb and utilize only a small part of what we hear each day.

What determines whether you sit up, pay attention, and actually listen to something? Frequently, it has to be information that's new. If you've heard something many times before, the chances are you'll tune out. The information also has to seem relevant, or important, to you. That is, you must think it's useful to you in school, in extracurricular activities, at your part-time job, or in your social relationships.

"Our reason for listening determines how we listen."

—Marion Geddes, listening expert

One way to improve your listening skills is to find something in what's being said that can help you or that seems relevant to you. Suppose you're sitting in class listening to a lecture. Instead of tuning out because it isn't your favorite subject, ask yourself the following questions: Is there any information here that I might need to be successful in a job or in college? Is there something that I didn't know before that seems interesting to me? Do I need this information to pass a test in the course and to get a good grade? If you can answer yes to any or all of those questions, it's likely to make you a better listener.

Another way to improve your listening skills is to focus on the big picture. You can't remember everything your teachers say.

There's just too much of it. So you have to learn to concentrate on what's most important. This includes only the main ideas and the important details. But how do you select what's important from what isn't? That's where effective listening comes in. By learning how to recognize the patterns in what your teachers say, you can start to figure out what's worth remembering.

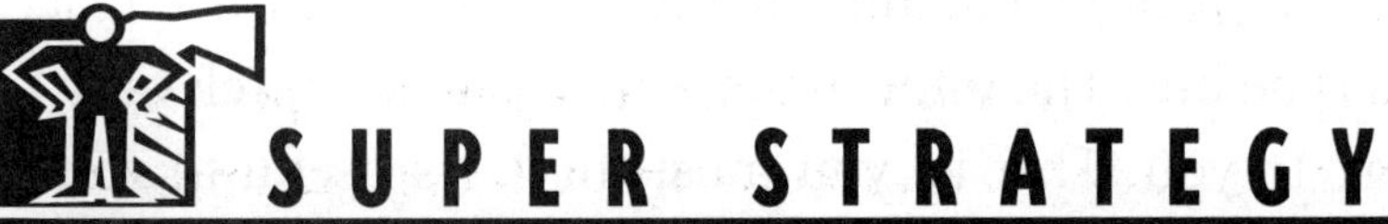

SUPER STRATEGY

FINDING THE LISTENING PATTERNS

Human beings like to make sense of things. As you sift through a large body of material, you probably try to organize it in your mind according to specific structures, or patterns. This is the approach you use in outlining a paper. You take all kinds of data and put it together in a logical pattern that will be understandable to your reader. Teachers do the same thing when they present information in class. They communicate information in a logical pattern that students can understand. If you know the pattern your teachers are using, you'll have a much easier time listening for the important information and remembering it. There are several types of patterns that occur over and over.

- **<u>Analyzing a process.</u> Suppose you're listening to a teacher explain how to conduct an experiment with seawater. The teacher might introduce the process with a topic sentence: "Today we're going to analyze the contents of seawater." This topic sentence tells you what he's going to be talking about. If you're taking notes, you might write down the heading:**

Analyzing Seawater. After introducing the topic, the teacher would probably begin talking about the steps necessary to carry out the process successfully. Each step usually starts with a key word: "First...second...third...." or "*Begin* by doing this...*then* do that....*next*...*finally*...." The key words in the pattern tip you off to the important information, which is presented chronologically. If you want to do the experiment correctly, you have to remember each of the steps and execute them in the proper chronological order.

- Historical chronology. You can listen for a similar type of pattern in social studies to present the key dates that comprise a significant historical event, such as a war or a social movement.

  Your teacher introduces the event—the Spanish-American War, for example. Then she discusses each of the important milestones in chronological order. "In 1898, the war began after the sinking of the American battleship *Maine*...." Linking the date together with the important incident is essential if you want to understand the cause of the war. So you must listen for the pattern of dates followed by events. And if you're taking notes, make sure you jot down the essential dates and what happened on each date.

- Comparison and contrast. This is a common pattern that occurs again and again in presenting information. Your teacher begins this way: "The presidential system in the United States and the parliamentary system in Great Britain have some similarities as well as some important differences." If you're listening closely, the key words similarities and differences should immediately tell you that the teacher is going to compare and contrast the two political systems. In your notes, you could make two headings: *United States* and *Great Britain.* Under each one, the teacher discusses several categories, one at a time. For example, he says: "Let's look first at the chief executive in each system....." then he lists the similarities, followed by the differences. Next he talks about the legislative branch. You could make a subheading for each category and include the important details of each in your notes.

- Cause and effect. This pattern might begin very simply. For instance, your teacher says: "There are many causes for the high divorce rate in the United States. Let's look at each of them...." Immediately you make a heading in your notes, titled *The high divorce rate in the United States.* Underneath, you list the various causes that your teacher presents. Some cause-and-effect patterns are a little different. Your teacher begins this way: "Many scientists believe that one of the major problems confronting the world is global warming. Today, we'll look at some of the factors that may lead to this problem." Then she lists the factors. Or your teacher introduces a single cause, then looks at a series of effects. Your teacher says: "Cigarette smoking can lead to a number of serious illnesses." Then she talks about each of the illnesses and discusses their relationship to smoking.

- Key elements. This pattern often consists of a large general category followed by its specific characteristics. Your teacher says: "Let's spend a few minutes talking about the characteristics of mammals." or "A short story has several essential elements." These words should tip you off to what's coming next—a discussion of the key elements. Sometimes the teacher may present them in a specific order, such as most important to least important. By recognizing the pattern, you can anticipate what's going to follow. This makes listening for the important information much easier.

If the listener can make a guess as to the sort of thing that is going to be said next, he will be much more likely to perceive it and understand it well."

—Penny Ur, Listening Expert

LISTENING FOR WORDS AND INFLECTIONS

By becoming more aware of language patterns, you become more skilled as a listener. By hearing certain words, such as **causes** or **similarities**, you can predict what's likely to follow, which helps you know what to listen for. Other words provide critical cues about what's important too. A partial list includes:

central	**chief**	**conclusion**	**critical**
crucial	**finally**	**first**	**foremost**
important	**key**	**leading**	**least**
main	**next**	**number one**	**second/secondary**
several	**significant**	**top priority**	**third**

In addition to the words they use, speakers also tell you what's important by the way they use inflection in their voice. If a speaker emphasizes a certain idea by raising her voice level, she wants you to pay particular attention to what she's saying. Some speakers lower their voice for emphasis. This forces you to strain so you can hear what the speaker is saying. As a result we have to focus even more closely on what the person is saying.

BODY LANGUAGE

Effective listening involves more than your ears. You must also use your eyes to watch the speaker's body language. Body language provides clues about what may be particularly important. Have you ever watched a television show or a videotape without the sound? You can often tell a great deal about what the speakers are saying by simply watching their gestures and facial expressions. Teachers rely on body language, too, as they deliver information in class. They use their hands or their arms to add greater emphasis to their ideas. Perhaps your teacher pumps an arm in the air to show that something he's saying is especially significant. Or if he's going to present three reasons to explain why an event occurred, he may raise a hand and put up three fingers for greater emphasis. This means that he wants you to remember what he's going to say.

A teacher's facial expressions often say as much as his words. They can provide extra clues that enable you to read more meaning into his statements. With a raised eyebrow or a shake of the head, a teacher can underscore his most important ideas. That's all the more reason to "listen" carefully not only to what's being spoken but also to what's being expressed through facial expressions and body language.

EFFECTIVE CLASSROOM LISTENING

As you sit in class, here are some things to keep in mind that will make you a better listener:

- *Don't give up.* Just because the information may seem difficult, don't stop listening. Concentrate as hard as you can and try to understand what your teacher is saying. Don't be afraid to ask questions if you don't grasp a concept.
- *Look for the cues.* Remember, your teacher uses patterns to present information. Try to spot the key words that tip you off to the organizational structure. Listen for key words that tell you whether an idea is particularly important.
- *Use more than your ears.* Listening is more than just an auditory experience. Your eyes enable you to see gestures and facial

You can often tell a great deal about what the speakers are saying by simply watching their gestures and facial expressions.

expressions that may provide significant clues about the teacher's message.

- *Put yourself in the teacher's shoes.* This means pay attention and give the teacher the courtesy of listening. If you were the one standing in front of the class, you wouldn't want to see students daydreaming or talking to each other.
- *Resist distractions.* Don't waste time looking out the window and daydreaming. Some teachers lecture on material that is not covered anywhere else. This may be the only opportunity you have to get the information. So it's important to listen carefully.

"The one who listens is the one who understands."

—Old Proverb

CONVERSATIONS

Conversations usually aren't as well structured as classroom presentations. Although the speaker may know what she wants to say, she may not have thought about her exact words very carefully. You've been in situations like that yourself. Perhaps it takes you awhile to get to the point. You use a lot of meaningless words, such as *um* and *ah* and *like*. You begin a sentence only to hesitate halfway through as another idea comes into your head. Then you start a new sentence and head off in another direction. If you're listening to someone who speaks this way, it can be difficult to follow what she is saying.

"When people speak naturally they know what they want to say. But they decide how they are going to say it as they are speaking."

—Marion Geddes

In the following example, the editor of a school newspaper is talking with her staff.

> "I know all of us want to make this an extremely good issue. And I've looked at the ideas for the inside pages and they're really great. I mean, they're some of the best... um....The sports articles are very interesting. Gee, Bill, I didn't know the baseball game the other day was so close. Nancy...ah...that article on the school public speaking program will get a lot of attention. And I guess that's what I want to spend some time talking about. How we can be sure to get everybody's attention. It has to start on the front page. The front page is the most important part of the paper. So that's what I want to tell you. We have to come up with some better ideas for the articles on the front page. That's where we make or break the paper. Do you have any suggestions?"

Notice how the editor meanders all over the place trying to get to the main point. She starts in one place, then begins another idea. She punctuates her sentences with meaningless words. She repeats certain words, such as *attention.* And she doesn't really get to her main point until the end. This is the way many people speak in normal conversation. They may know where their words are going, but the listeners aren't always so sure. If you happen to be the listener, what can you do to make it easier to figure out the message? Here are a few things to keep in mind.

- *Be patient.* Sometimes it takes a few moments before the speaker actually gets to the point. While the speaker is talking, try to concentrate. Don't daydream or become impatient.
- *Pay attention to key words.* Experts tell us that we tend to repeat words in conversation that are really important to us. The editor in the previous example repeated *attention* and *front page.* As you listen, pay particular attention to words that the speaker says more than once. Also look for key words from our earlier list: important, crucial, top priority, first, second, etc.
- *Pay attention to phrases; they're important.* Speakers often signal their main point with certain common phrases. They may begin with a word, such as *so.* "So that's what I want to say." The word *so* often indicates that the speaker is summing up everything he has said so far and making an important point. Or the speaker may use a phrase such as "I want you to remember", or "I think this is what we have to do."
- *Don't interrupt.* Give the speaker an opportunity to say what she wants to say. Don't cut in partway through her message and interrupt. Unless you give the speaker a chance to finish, you may never find out what she's trying to tell you—especially if she doesn't deliver her main point until the end.

- *Don't Assume.* One of the biggest errors that listeners make is to assume they know where the speaker is going. The fact is that you can think much faster than most people talk. The average speaker talks at about 160 words per minute; you process ideas at three times that rate. So it's easy to be bored listening to the speaker and to jump ahead, thinking you know what the speaker will say. As a result, you stop listening and may make the wrong assumption.
- *Tune out static.* Background sounds and other conversations can sometimes get in the way of effective listening. Your internal static—boredom and daydreaming—can disrupt the communication too. Concentrate on the speaker and try to tune out the distractions.
- *Don't forget body language.* Watching the speaker's body language will help you evaluate the validity of what he's saying. Does he look you in the eye? Do his eyes dart around while he's speaking? This may indicate that the speaker is hiding something. Some speakers wring their hands or fiddle with their jewelry. This may be a sign of nervousness. Ask yourself why the speaker is nervous. Perhaps he's just upset. Or he may be concealing something important from you.

THE LISTENER'S BODY LANGUAGE

Good listeners focus on the speaker's verbal and nonverbal cues to understand the meaning of the message. As a listener, you should be aware of the nonverbal signals that you're sending while someone is talking to you. With your body language, you have the ability to help the speaker and encourage her to talk. Or you can present a physical barrier that makes communication extremely difficult.

YOUR NONVERBAL CUES

THUMBS UP

Do look at the speaker and indicate your interest in what is being said.

Do nod your head as the speaker talks. This shows that you are listening and understanding what he's saying.

Keep your arms at your sides or fold your hands while the speaker talks. This is an open position that invites conversation.

Keep your posture erect while you sit or stand. This demonstrates that you're alert and listening to the speaker.

THUMBS DOWN

Don't look away or up in the air. This suggests that you're bored or uninterested.

Don't stare at the speaker with no expression on your face. This mode of listening only makes him feel self-conscious.

Don't sit or stand with your arms folded across your chest. This is a closed position that prevents communication.

Don't slouch while the speaker is talking. The speaker may feel that you're tired and bored.

MEMORY TRICK: FALL

Whenever you listen, remember these four simple principles:

FIND something in what the speaker is saying that's relevant to you. That way, you're more likely to pay attention.

ALWAYS focus on the main ideas. You can't possibly recall everything the speaker said.

LISTEN for the patterns in the way the material is organized and presented. It will be easier to understand and remember.

LOOK at the speaker's body language and encourage the speaker with your own non-verbal cues.

LISTENING SKILLS ON A PART-TIME JOB

Working after school at a part-time job is one way you prepare for the world of work after graduation. The job you do now probably won't be what you'll be doing later. But this work experience can teach you some of the skills you'll need to be successful. These include skills such as teamwork, following directions, and knowing how to deal with customers. All of these rely in part on effective listening.

The importance of listening begins when you first apply for a job. In an employment interview, listening skills can spell the dif-

ference between being hired and not being hired. The interviewer will ask you a series of questions. She may want to know where else you've worked, what training you've received, and why you want this particular job. Don't assume you know what the speaker is asking and begin to answer before she finishes her question. Interviewers don't like being interrupted before they stop talking. Furthermore, if you provide inappropriate information in answer to the interviewer's question, you will make a bad impression and possibly not get the job. While the interviewer is talking, indicate that you understand the question by nodding your head and saying "uh huh" or "I see." Once the interviewer has finished, you can begin your answer.

Remember to watch your body language during the interview. Try to make eye contact with the interviewer as much as possible. If you look off into space or down at the floor while the interviewer is talking, she may assume that you are not paying attention or—worse yet—are bored with the interview and not interested in the job. Perhaps you have the nervous habit of drumming on the table as you sit across from someone who is talking to you. Unfortunately, this gives the impression that you're impatient or not interested in what the speaker is saying. If you act this way during a job interview, you're not likely to be hired.

Some job applicants also have the unpleasant habit of slouching in the chair during the interview. That's the kind of body language that says to an interviewer: "I'm sloppy and undisciplined." Employers are not looking for those types of people.

Remember, the job interview is the first impression you make on an employer. You want it to be positive, not negative. This means you must know how to communicate effectively—which not only involves speaking but listening too.

Experts point out that we listen only to about 25 percent of what someone is telling us.

FOLLOWING DIRECTIONS ON THE JOB

On a new job, you're likely to encounter situations that you've never seen before, and you're likely to be asked to carry out new tasks according to specific step-by-step procedures. Generally, these steps must be followed exactly to ensure that the task is done correctly. Otherwise, you are likely to make a mistake—one which might prove very costly to your company in terms of lost dollars, lost time, and lost customer satisfaction. Effective listening is a critical skill that can enable you to follow directions successfully.

- Listen to all of the steps. If a supervisor is explaining how to deal with customer complaints, don't assume you've heard this procedure before at your last job and think you know exactly what to do. Complaints may be handled differently on your new job. Pay close attention to everything you are being told so you can carry out the procedure correctly.
- Ask questions. If you don't understand something, ask. Chances are you're not the only person who can't figure out what the speaker is saying. Sometimes you may feel foolish raising your hand and asking what you think may be a "dumb" question. But you'll feel a lot more ridiculous if you make a mistake later and are criticized by your supervisor in front of your co-workers.
- Look for the logic. Each of the steps in a procedure is usually there for a reason. Your employer didn't include them just to make life difficult for you. The steps are based on past experience—and frequently have been derived the hard way, by

someone making a mistake. Try to understand the reason for every step and why the steps follow each other in a specific order. This will help you carry them out correctly.

- Take notes. On a new job, you get a lot of information thrown at you very quickly. It's almost impossible to keep everything in your head. If you're afraid you won't remember something, write it down. Keep the instructions with you as you begin to perform the procedure. Once you've done the procedure a few times and become familiar with it, you probably won't need the written directions at your side any longer.

LISTENING TO CUSTOMERS

Customers are the lifeblood of any company. Without them, the organization quickly goes out of business. Customers pay your salary and the salaries of everyone who works with you. Many jobs—clerks and salespeople in stores, waiters and waitresses in restaurants, checkout people in supermarkets, administrative assistants and receptionists in offices—involve dealing directly with customers. When customers deal with a business, they expect prompt, courteous service. In order to give customers what they want, you have to listen to them carefully.

In an employment interview, listening skills can spell the difference between being hired and not being hired.

- Adjust to the customer. You may be a person who's very direct—someone who gets to the point right away. Some customers are this way too. If you're working in a store, they'll come up to you and tell you what they're looking for immediately. They don't have time to beat around the bush. But other customers are different. They're a little more reluctant to ask for help. And it takes them a few moments to finally get around to the purpose of their conversation. Earlier, we pointed out that normal conversation often includes hesitations and filler words, and the speaker may not make his point until the end. Many customers act the same way. So you must be patient and adjust yourself to their style of speaking.

- Give the customer some help. One of the best ways to make a customer feel more comfortable is through your body language. Smiling encourages a customer to speak to you. Looking directly at a customer signals that you are interested in what she is saying. Nodding your head says that you are paying attention and want her to continue talking. After the customer has finished making a request, you can paraphrase what she has said to make sure you understand it correctly. For example: Suppose you're working in a bookstore. A customer comes in looking for a book she heard about on the radio, but she can't remember the title or the author. You might say: "It sounds as though you're looking for that new thriller [mention the name],which just came into the store yesterday." If she says yes, then you can show her to the mystery section. In this situation, you are paraphrasing what the customer said—stating the meaning in a shortened form—to verify that you understand it clearly. Paraphrasing is a useful technique whenever you listen to someone. It's another way of showing that you're interested in what the speaker is saying as well as assuring yourself that you understand her message accurately.

- Don't make snap judgments. Many customers dress differently than you do. When they speak, it may be with a foreign accent or with a heavy regional twang. Perhaps they speak more slowly than you do, or much faster. It's easy to jump to a negative judgment about someone based simply on the way he looks or how he sounds. As a result, you may not listen to him very carefully. Remember, customers deserve your attention. They're the reason your employer is in business, so you should listen when they speak.
- Tune in over the telephone. Much of your contact with customers may occur over the telephone. Since the speaker is not standing in front of you, her facial expression cannot give you any clues as to what she's feeling—upset, angry, uncomfortable. So you have to listen carefully to her words and the inflection in her voice. Sometimes it's difficult dealing with customers who are not very pleasant. Try putting yourself in their place for a few moments. Listen to what they say and, if possible, empathize with their feelings. A sympathetic ear on the other end of the phone may be all they need to feel better.

GET THE MOST OUT OF MEETINGS

Much of the work that gets done in organizations today occurs in meetings. Orientation meetings introduce new employees to their company by describing all of its different departments and what they do. Team meetings involve employees who are working together on a project and need to coordinate their activities. Your supervisor may call a meeting of all part-time employees to discuss the schedule for the busy holiday season to ensure that enough people are available to handle the work. Whenever you sit in a meeting, your listening skills can prove especially valuable in helping you get the most out of the meeting. Try to remember these tips and apply them whether you're attending meetings at work or at school.

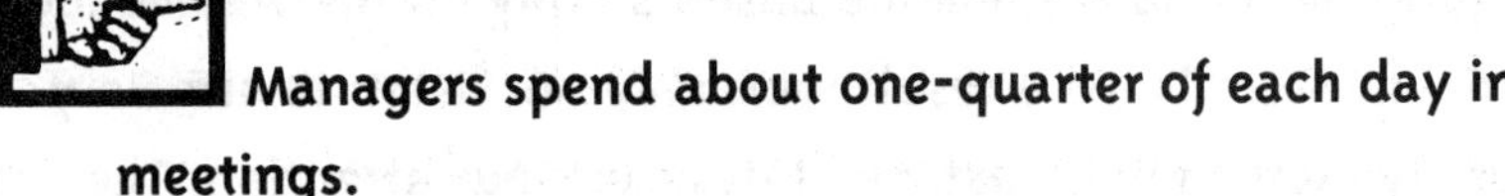

Managers spend about one-quarter of each day in meetings.

- Listen to the agenda. An agenda lists the major topics to be covered in the meeting. Generally, the meeting leader will review the agenda before anything else occurs. Listen carefully because the agenda will tell you what to expect during the meeting and will help you focus your attention on the key points to be discussed.
- Don't daydream. Some meetings can be quite lengthy, especially if the speakers tend to be long-winded. But if you start to daydream, you may miss something important. Try to concentrate as much as possible. Look for something that's relevant to you—this is the best way to avoid losing your concentration.
- Avoid hasty decisions. Sometimes you'll be listening to a speaker and find yourself disagreeing with what he says. At this point, you might want to stop listening. You decide that he doesn't know what he's talking about anyway, so why pay attention any longer. Unfortunately, you may have jumped to a hasty conclusion. Give the speaker the benefit of the doubt and let him finish before you make any judgments. You may discover that he has more to say than you thought.
- Listen, don't speak. When you disagree with someone, you might be tempted to interrupt and immediately state your own

opinions. Not only is this discourteous, it also prevents you from listening to the speaker's presentation all the way through. Control yourself and wait your turn. You'd want the speaker to treat you the same way.

- Don't trust your memory. You can't always expect to remember all the important items that were covered at a meeting. So take a few notes. Don't try to write down everything. You don't need all that information anyway. Just jot down the main ideas to help you remember them. That way, you'll avoid writer's cramp and missing important points.

FOR REVIEW

1. What are several different categories of listening situations?
2. How can you improve your selective listening?
3. What patterns do teachers use to present information in class?
4. How can you become a better listener in the classroom?
5. How do conversations differ from classroom presentations?
6. What skills will improve your ability to listen in conversations?
7. How does your body language affect a speaker?
8. How can you use listening skills in a job interview?
9. What should you do to improve your ability to follow directions?
10. How can you use listening skills in your dealings with customers?
11. What listening skills are valuable in meetings?

ON-THE-JOB TERMINOLOGY

One way of becoming a better listener is to have a broader understanding of some of the new terms you might hear on your after-school job. Here are a few terms that might be important to know.

absenteeism: the number of employees that are absent from work

accounts payable: the money owed by the employer to suppliers and other businesses

accounts receivable: the money owed to the employer by customers

assets: what the company owns, such as equipment used for its business

bottom line: the company's profits or losses. When someone asks, "What's the bottom line?" it often means how much is the company going to gain or lose by doing something

budget: the money a business or department has available to operate

cash flow: the cash coming into a business from customers

cross-training: training an employee to do more than one job

database: a computer file consisting of related information organized into fields and records. Databases can usually be searched or sorted by field, such as the last name of a customer in a database of sales records

flextime: a work schedule other than the usual 9-to-5 day

fringe benefits: benefits other than salary, such as paid holidays and health insurance

inventory: the items that are available to sell to customers

job sharing: situation in which two people share one job

management by objectives (MBO): a process of setting goals for employees

marketing plan: the strategy for marketing a company's products

minimum wage: the lowest salary an employee can be paid under the law

on-the-job training (OJT): learning the job by actually doing it while being supervised by an experienced employee

overtime: hours above and beyond the usual work day

overhead: the fixed expenses of a business, such as rent

petty cash: the cash available for small, incidental expenses, such as snacks for employees or cab fare

seniority: a way of determining a person's position in an organization based on length of service

team building: a training program to develop strong teamwork among employees so they can work together on projects smoothly

turnover: the number of employees being hired and leaving

8 INFORMATION MANAGEMENT

You are part of the generation that has grown up in the "information age."

Surrounded by information in school and out, you need to know how to find information, deal with it, and make use of it. This chapter will show you how to use one of the greatest repositories of information—the library.

IN THIS CHAPTER YOU WILL LEARN:

- **how a library is organized**
- **how to use card and electronic catalogs**
- **what resources a library or media center has to offer**
- **how to use microfilm and microfiche**
- **what the Internet can do for you**
- **how to approach research as a problem to solve**
- **how to keep track of the information you gather**
- **how to write a research paper**

HOW A LIBRARY IS ORGANIZED

To some people, libraries are mysterious and overwhelming places. With a little help and patience, however, anyone can find his way around a library. After all, libraries are organized so that people can locate the materials they need.

To begin with, libraries separate fiction books from nonfiction, and they usually have special areas for reference books, magazines, and other materials. Fiction books are arranged on shelves alphabetically by the authors' last names.

Most libraries organize their nonfiction materials using one of two systems: the Library of Congress classification or the Dewey decimal system classification. Some very large libraries use LOC, but most town and school libraries use Dewey.

Librarian Melvil Dewey designed a system for classifying and arranging nonfiction books in 1876. He divided nonfiction into ten major subject categories, listed below.

000-099	**General Works**
100-199	**Philosophy, Psychology**
200-299	**Religion**
300-399	**Social Sciences (including Education)**
400-499	**Language**
500-599	**Pure Sciences (including Mathematics)**
600-699	**Applied Arts and Sciences (Technology)**
700-799	**Fine Arts, Recreation**
800-899	**Literature**
900-999	**History, Geography, Biography**

Within each category are subcategories, indicated by individual numbers. For example, in the Social Science section (including Education), books on general study skills are assigned 371, and standardized test review books are assigned 378.

Libraries also assign each book a letter-number combination based on the book's author. This appears on a line below the Dewey classification number. On the shelf, all college test review books with the number 378.1664 are arranged alphabetically, according to author. Libraries also put a letter *before* the Dewey number when the book is in a special section: R (or Ref) for Reference, J for Juvenile, Y for Young Adult.

THE SECRETS OF CATALOG SYSTEMS

You don't have to memorize the Dewey numbers to find a book. The library's catalog system makes it easy. Whether the library has a card system or an electronic system, you can search for a book three ways: by title, by author, or by subject.

In a card system, each book has three cards: an author card, a title card, and a subject card. These are arranged alphabetically in separate author, title, and subject catalogs. Each card indicates the book's **call number:** the Dewey decimal number plus the author letter-number combination. With this call number, you can usually find the book on the proper shelf.

If you cannot find a book, it may be misshelved. First see if it is hidden behind the row of books where it should be. Then look at nearby books and shelves. If you still cannot find it, ask a librarian to help you; perhaps the book is sitting on a cart waiting to be reshelved.

Many libraries now have electronic systems: You search for a book using a computer. The computer tells you step-by-step how to search by title, author, or subject. When you find the book you want, write down the call number; some systems even print out a list of books and call numbers.

The computer also tells you if the book is currently checked out and when it is due. You can ask the library to hold it for you when it has been returned. Often libraries share resources—you can borrow books available at other libraries indicated in the database through Inter-Library Loan (ILL). The library that has the book you are seeking will send it to the library you are using.

Whether the library has a card system or an electronic system, you can search for a book three ways: by title, by author, or by subject.

THE LIBRARY AS A MEDIA CENTER

The modern library is often appropriately referred to as a *media center*. A library conveys information through the *media* of books, newspapers, magazines, journals, audiotapes, videotapes, computers, CD-ROMS, microfilm, microfiche, map collections, photo collections, and more. Each of these is a potential resource.

The library is a wonderful place when you need to know *more* about a subject. Perhaps you would like to deepen your understanding of a topic discussed in class or presented in your textbook. Or perhaps you need more information for an assignment; many school projects require research. The library can help you find the information you need to:

- develop your position for a debate
- write an informative or a persuasive essay
- prepare an oral presentation
- critique a literary work
- design a science project
- write a research paper

THE REFERENCE SECTION

Many of the resources you need will be found in the library's reference section. Reference materials usually cannot be checked out. Become familiar with what your library's reference section has to offer. In general, a library's reference section will include:

- *Dictionaries.* Besides the usual English language dictionaries, you may find specialized dictionaries of foreign languages, science, and many other subjects. There are also dictionaries of synonyms, called thesauruses.
- *Encyclopedias.* Encyclopedias usually have multiple volumes of alphabetically arranged entries on many topics. Each volume's spine indicates the letters it covers. There are also specialized encyclopedias covering such areas as science and geography.
- *Atlases.* Atlases are not just collections of maps. They contain a wealth of information on topics such as history, politics, religions, economics, and languages. There are also atlases that specialize in topics such as wildlife and ethnic diversity.
- *Collections.* Reference sections also may contain collections of maps, photographs, and art. Some of these items can be checked out and used in written reports or oral presentations.
- *Almanacs, yearbooks, record books, and fact books.* Editions of these books are usually published each year. They provide statistics and information in many areas, including government, sports, and entertainment.
- *Biographical profile books.* These reference books contain brief biographies of people, living and dead. Some cover people in all fields; others specialize in a particular field, such as authors.
- *Indexes and guides to periodicals, newspapers, and journals.* These references list articles that appear in magazines, newspapers, and journals. Entries are by subject headings; listings indicate an article's title and author, name of publication, volume number, date, and page numbers. Some indexes contain *abstracts,* or summaries of the original articles. In most libraries, recent magazines can be checked out.

ELECTRONIC REFERENCES

There are electronic versions of many of the kinds of references listed above. The library may have some in their on-line database and others in CD-ROM. Using these electronic references is relatively simple: The computer will take you through a step-by-step process. Librarians willingly instruct people on an as-needed basis or in formal classes.

A great advantage of electronic references is that they are likely to be current. CD-ROM databases are updated frequently, and some on-line databases are updated every day.

Many libraries also have computerized guides to newspapers and periodicals. A search by subject, author, or title produces a list of articles with a brief description of each. This will help you decide if you want to obtain an article. Some systems are equipped to show the full text of selected articles on the monitor; some will even print out articles. Or if the library subscribes to the magazine, the issue may be available or you may view it on microform.

USING MICROFILM AND MICROFICHE

Because libraries do not have enough room to keep the actual copies of newspapers and magazines for very long, most transfer them to microforms such as *film* or *fiche*. A photographic process miniaturizes an issue of the newspaper or magazine, and this film can be viewed on a monitor of a special machine that enlarges it. *Microfilm* is a reel of such film, and *microfiche* is a card-sized flat sheet.

The machines and microforms are usually kept in a special section of the library. There are rules concerning their use; often the machines have to be reserved, and usually a librarian gets the film from its storage place.

The librarian will show you how to use the machine. It may

Many libraries now have computers with modems with access to the Net.

take a little time to become adept at scrolling the film, but soon you will be comfortable doing it.

Some machines are designed to make a full-size photocopy for a small price. Those machines are usually equipped with a coin box; some may accept dollar bills. But if you plan to make many copies, it would be wise to bring a supply of change.

THE INTERNET AS A REFERENCE TOOL

Another important reference tool is the Internet, home of the World Wide Web. Many libraries now have computers with modems with access to the Net. Searching the Net is as simple as typing in the subject in one of the standard search engines, such as *Yahoo.*

You can get instructions on how to use the Internet at the library, or ask an experienced friend to show you. And ask friends, librarians, and teachers to recommend good sites for the kind of information you need. Libraries also have directories listing Web site addresses by subject.

You may want to "visit" Capitol Hill to follow activities in Congress, research current events at news services, observe ongoing science projects at national institutes, take a multimedia tour of the solar system, or view art at virtual museums. You can also tap into networks to explore postings by experts in many fields, or you can consult with experts via E-mail.

There is no end to the information available on the Net. In fact, students often mention the opposite problem: There is *too much* information available! Teachers, on the other hand, are concerned about *accuracy* on the Net. Anyone can post information on a Web site. It is crucial to judge the reliability of the source.

First determine if the Web site is maintained by an expert in the field: You can probably trust information about Congress from the nation's largest publisher of congressional directories. But if you cannot be sure of the Net source, cross-check information with one or more print or electronic sources. Then, as with any source, judge the quality of the Web site's information. For example, examine it for consistency and logical reasoning and be alert for bias and unsupported generalizations.

MEMORY TRICK: PISE

Do you dread research projects because you don't know where to begin and what to do? The best approach may be one with which you are already familiar: Treat a research project as a problem to solve. Remember **PISE**, the four steps to problem solving described in Chapter Two.

PROBLEM. Identify the problem. Identify the topic; formulate a question or state a thesis. Decide what information you need to answer the question or support your position.

INFORMATION. Gather appropriate information. Consider possible sources: Skim each source to decide if it is relevant;

evaluate the quality of the source; select or reject the source. Record any appropriate information.

SOLVE. Use the information to solve the problem. Organize your information from all sources. Analyze it logically to reach a conclusion. Present information in the form (written, graphic, oral) that satisfies the requirements of the assignment.

EVALUATE. Evaluate the solution. Determine if your research product answers the original question or effectively supports your position. Determine which research techniques were most effective.

SUPER STRATEGY

KEEPING TRACK OF INFORMATION

If you are doing research as part of an assignment, it is important to organize the information that you gather. Although some students use a notebook, most prefer using index cards to record important information. There are two types of note cards.

BIBLIOGRAPHY CARDS

Make a separate bibliography card for every source you consider—even those you are not positive you will use. Number each card in the upper right-hand corner. The card should include all the publication information you will need to identify the book and create a formal bibliography if required.

- **For a *book,* include the author, title, publisher, city of publication and date. Also record the call number.**
- **If the source is an *anthology,* include the name of the editor as well as the title and author of the individual piece you are using, plus publication information.**

- If the source is an *encyclopedia,* treat it as an anthology; include the volume number.
- If the source is a *newspaper, journal,* or *periodical,* include the author (if known), the title of the article, the publication name, the volume number, the date and the page numbers. Also note if the source was in microfilm or microfiche.
- If the source is a *computer* database, Web site, or software, note as much detail as possible, including the distributor or manufacturer.
- If you use sources from more than one library, be sure to note the name of the library on each card. Also note any information about the source's location in the library. This information will save you time if you need to find the source later.

INFORMATION CARDS

As you gather appropriate information, make notes on index cards. Later, arrange the cards in a logical way that explains your topic. Here are some guidelines for recording the information you gather.

- Each card should cover only one idea. At the top of the card, put a subject heading to identify this main idea.
- Summarize the information. Don't copy large amounts *verbatim* (word for word); put the information in your own words, or *paraphrase* it.
- If you do select a particular word, phrase, sentence, or passage to

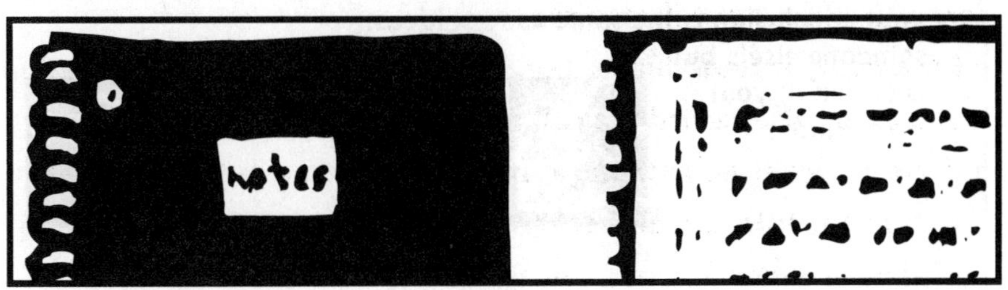

quote, be very careful to indicate this as a direct quotation: use quotation marks *and* write the word QUOTE on the card.

- Also write comments that indicate your reaction to the information: whether you agree with the opinion of the author; if this fact is a strong argument in support of your position or thesis, etc.
- Identify the source for each card with the bibliography card number *and* the author's last name. (Do not use the number alone; it is easy to make a mistake.) Record exactly which pages of the source were used for the information *on that card.* Use this information to give proper credit to the author when you write your paper.

RULES OF EVIDENCE

THUMBS UP
It is not plagiarism if

- the information is a generally known fact, such as the Pacific is the deepest ocean.
- you use an idiomatic or common saying, such as "Haste makes waste."
- you use quotation marks and credit the original source.
- you combine paraphrases of the original with partial quotes and credit the source.
- your conclusion is the same as someone else's but is stated in your own words.

THUMBS DOWN
It is plagiarism if you don't give credit when

- you copy another author's words—even if you use a different order.
- you use another author's examples.
- you copy an illustration, diagram, or chart.
- you present another author's original theory as your own.
- you extensively copy another author's exact progression of ideas.

SUPER TACTIC

WRITING A RESEARCH PAPER

The process of writing a research paper follows the same basic steps as writing an English essay described in Chapter Four.

1. Identify a topic and define your message. Teachers often assign a general topic, or provide a list of topics from which students may choose. Select a topic that genuinely interests you, then decide what you want to say about it. Defining your message will focus your research and writing. Even if it is an assigned topic, personalize it by taking a position; your writing will be more interesting. If you cannot narrow your focus, proceed to the next step.

2. Brainstorm for ideas. Professionals sometimes call this freewriting or stream of consciousness. Jot down any ideas, words, or phrases that interest you. Include questions: What do you want to know about the topic? Think about your message: What do you want the reading *audience* to know about your topic? Don't worry about spelling, punctuation, or using complete sentences. The idea is to put down your thoughts as they come to you.

   Examine your notes to identify several main ideas; use these as headings and group other related ideas under them. Decide which relationships to explore. Begin to think about the order of presentation that will best develop your message. This will result in a rough outline to guide your research.
3. Conduct your research. Use general resources first to build your background knowledge. Start with dictionaries and encyclopedias. Then consult more specific sources to find interesting details and evidence to support your position.

Take advantage of all the resources the library has to offer, but don't be overwhelmed. You don't need to read every book on your topic. Skim the table of contents, index, and chapter titles to see if a book is relevant to your thesis and scan for the information you need. Then take careful notes as described earlier in this chapter. Don't forget to indicate your reaction to the information. This will help you with your writing later.

Don't forget to make bibliography cards for every source you use and be sure to properly identify the source and page numbers for every information card you write. Use a subject heading and put only one idea on each card. Be concise and paraphrase the information you read. Be careful when recording quotes. The time you take now to record proper notes will be well spent making writing a much easier task.

4. Develop a final outline. Once you think you have enough information, spread your cards out in front of you. Consult your rough outline. Write each major outline point on a new card; put your information cards in a column under the proper point. Read through the cards to determine if you have enough information for each point. If you do not, make a note to obtain more data for that point. You do not necessarily need to find new sources; now that you know exactly what information is needed, select your most likely sources and scan for that information.

   When you are finished gathering information, you may decide there is an additional aspect of your topic that you would like to include. If it is relevant to your thesis, simply add it at the appropriate place in your outline. Make other necessary revisions in your outline at this time: add points, delete points, or change the order of points. Then flesh out the supporting points too. Try to include support from three sources for each major point. Reorder your note cards to reflect this final outline.

5. Write the first draft. State your thesis clearly in the first paragraph. Summarize the major points you will make to support it. This paragraph may also include introductory material to set the background and to interest the reader.

   Proceed to discuss each major point in your outline, using the information on your note cards. Be sure to explain relationships and show their significance to your thesis. Put each major point and its supporting details in a separate section of your paper. Create a heading for each section based on the major point; you may also use subheadings to reflect supporting details.

   Your conclusion should restate your thesis and summarize how each major point relates to it. This section should not include any new information. If something significant occurs to you, rework the main body of your paper to include it.

6. Revise the paper and type a final draft. If possible, have someone read your paper and make suggestions. Then carefully read your paper, section by section. Determine if you have provided adequate support for your thesis. Make sure that you have not left out important information and that your information is presented in a logical order. Use transitions to make your paper readable and understandable.

   Check to be sure you have made transitions between paragraphs, subsections, and sections. Your paper will be weaker if these are missing. Remember, *you* are now an expert on your topic; your reader needs to be shown how your points are related. A paper lacking in continuity will not seem logical in spite of good evidence and support. Reading your paper aloud will help you notice missing or awkward transitions.

   Finally, check for errors in grammar, punctuation, and spelling. Also check that you have followed exactly the format for footnotes and bibliography required by your teacher.

When you type the final copy, include a title page with your name as author. In the body of the paper, use one-inch margins all around; and number the pages. Use double spacing in the body and triple spacing between paragraphs. Place the completed paper in a binder, and turn in your paper on time.

Current word processing programs greatly simplify and expedite research paper preparation. It is to your advantage to become proficient in using computer-based word processors.

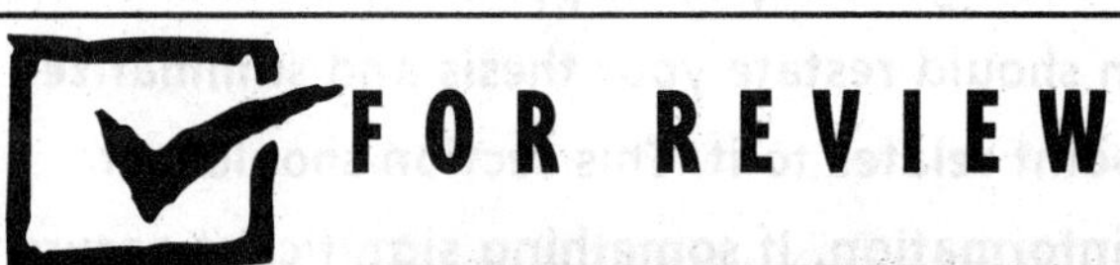

FOR REVIEW

1. How are fiction books arranged on library shelves?
2. What classification system does your library use?
3. What three kinds of cards are in a library's catalog system?
4. What are six examples of media available in most libraries?
5. What is a thesis statement?
6. What process would you use to ensure the accuracy of information obtained on the Internet?
7. What is the difference between the two kinds of note cards you would use to track the data your research produces?
8. What are five kinds of reference materials? Briefly describe each.

LIBRARY REFERENCE MATERIAL

The materials listed below are only a small representation of what may be available in your library. You will also find it useful to look at the books located on shelves near these materials. They are likely to be similar in content. Many may also be available on your library's computer.

ALMANACS, YEARBOOKS, FACT BOOKS

Facts On File. New York: Facts On File, 1940 — (weekly world news digests)

Famous First Facts. New York: H. W. Wilson, 1964 (single volume)

Guiness Book of World Records. New York: Sterling, and other publishers, 1962–

Information Please Almanac. Boston: Houghton Mifflin, 1947–

The World Almanac and Book of Facts. New York: Newspaper Enterprise Assn., 1868–

ATLASES

Use the most up-to-date atlas you can find; Hammond, Rand McNally, National Geographic, and others publish general and specialized atlases.

Atlas of the Universe. Chicago: Rand McNally, 1970

NASA Atlas of the Solar System. Cambridge: Cambridge Univ. Press, 1997

USA Today Sports Atlas. New York: Simon and Schuster, 1991

We the People: An Atlas of America's Ethnic Diversity. James Paul Allen and Eugene Turner. New York: Macmillan, 1988

BIOGRAPHY

American Men and Women of Science. New York: Bowker, 1982 (7 volumes)

Biography Index. New York: H. W. Wilson, 1947– (quarterly; cumulated annually)

Current Biography. New York: H. W. Wilson, 1940– (monthly; annual index of decade)

Twentieth-Century Authors. New York: H. W. Wilson, 1942 (supplement 1955)

Who's Who. London: Black, 1849– (annually; living persons)

Who's Who in America. Chicago: Marquis, 1899– (biennially)

Who's Who of American Women. Chicago: Marquis, 1958– (biennially)
Who Was Who (historical volumes of reprinted entries)

DICTIONARIES

Webster, Random House, Funk and Wagnalls, and others publish standard dictionaries. Use an unabridged dictionary for more information and the *Oxford English Dictionary* for the history of a word.

Dictionary of American Literary Characters. New York: Facts On File, 1990
Dictionary of Art Terms and Techniques. New York: Lewis, 1981
Dictionary of the History of Ideas. New York: Scribner's, 1974 (5 volumes)
Dictionary of Wars. George C. Kohn. New York: Facts On File, 1986
Harvard Dictionary of Music. Cambridge, Mass.: Harvard Univ. Press, 1969
Safire's New Political Dictionary. William Safire. New York: Random House, 1993

McGraw-Hill Dictionary of Scientific and Technical Terms. Illinois: McGraw-Hill, 1994

ENCYCLOPEDIAS

For serious academic work, use *Collier's Encyclopedia, Encyclopaedia Britannica,* or *Encyclopedia Americana* in the most recent edition available.

Encyclopedia of African-American Culture and History. New York: Macmillan, 1996
Encyclopedia of American History. New York: Harper and Row, 1976
Encyclopedia of World Facts and Dates. Gorton Carruth. New York: HarperCollins, 1993
Oxford Illustrated Encyclopedia of World History. New York: Oxford Univ. Press, 1988
The Reader's Encyclopedia. William R. Benet. New York: Crowell, 1965
Van Nostrand's Scientific Encyclopedia. New York: Van Nostrand Reinhold, 1976

INDEXES

These reference books are guides to sources such as books and periodicals. Generally, listings by subject headings provide publication information to help you find the sources. Abstracts and digests include a summary of the source cited.

Book Review Digest. New York: H. W. Wilson, 1905– (Monthly; annual cumulations)

Historical Abstracts, 1775–1945. Santa Barbara, Calif.: ABC-Clio Press, 1955–

National Newspaper Index. Menlo Park, Calif.: Information Access, 1979 (monthly updates; major newspapers)

Reader's Guide to Periodical Literature. New York: H. W. Wilson, 1905– (semimonthly; quarterly, annual, and biennial cumulations)

ELECTRONIC REFERENCES

Some of the above indexes, as well as the ones listed below, may be available on your library's computer.

Granger Poetry Index (poems by first or last line, subject, or title; full text)

Proquest (database of 580 magazines, journals, and newspapers from 1986–)

SIRS Researcher (database focusing on social issues; full-text articles)

SIRS Government Reporter (current and historical documents)

SIRS Rennaissance (focus on humanities)

INTERNET DIRECTORIES

Check your library's reference section for books listing Web site addresses.

The following selected addresses are from *The Internet Resource Directory for K-12 Teachers and Librarians, 97/98 Edition* by Elizabeth B. Miller, published in Englewood, Colo. by Libraries Unlimited Inc., 1998.

Art, Music, and Drama

The Metropolitan Museum of Art, New York City

http://www.metmuseum.org

The National Gallery of Art, Washington, D.C.

http://www.nga.gov

World Wide Arts Resources

http://wwar.com

Mammoth Music Meta-List from VIBE

http://www.vibe.com/vibe/mmm/music.html

Theater and Drama Resources from the WWW Virtual Library

http://www.brookes.ac.uk/VL/theatre/index.htm

Literature and Writing

Best Rated Educational Internet Sites

http://www.sofsource.com and

http://208.145.149.29/LearnResource/cchoice.htm

Nineteenth-Century American Women Writers.

http://www.clever.net/19cwww/home2.html

19th-Century British and Irish Authors

http://lang.nagoya-u.ac.jp/~matsuoka/19th-authors.html

The Writers' Workshop: On-line Resources for Writers

http://www.english.uiuc.edu/cws/wworkshop/writer.html

Math and Science

Best Rated Educational Internet Sites

http://208.145.149.29/LearnResource/cchoice.htm

Frequently Asked Questions in Mathematics

http://daisy.uwaterloo.ca/~alopez-o/math-faq/math-faq.html

History of Mathematics

http://www.groups.dcs.st-and.ac.uk:80/~history

Franklin Institute Virtual Science Museum (Philadelphia)

http://sln.fi.edu

Science Bytes

http://loki.ur.utk.edu/ut2kids

Smithsonian Institution's Natural History Web

http://nmnhwww.si.edu/nmnhweb.html

Social Studies

Best Rated Educational Internet Sites

http://208.145.149.29/LearnResource/cchoice.htm

The History Channel

http://www.historychannel.com

From Revolution to Reconstruction and What Happened Afterward

http://www.let.rug.nl/~welling/usa/revolution.html

National Museum of American History Home Page

http://www.siledu/nmah

Smithsonian Institution Home Page

HYPERLINK http://www.si.edu http://www.si.edu

PUBLIC SPEAKING

Suppose you had to stand up in front of a group of people and deliver a speech. How would you react? When Americans were asked about their attitude toward public speaking, a majority said they were extremely afraid of it. Indeed, a poll showed that Americans would rather do almost anything else. Most said they would choose to have a serious illness, experience financial problems, or even die. So if you're afraid of making a speech, you're not alone.

IN THIS CHAPTER, YOU'LL LEARN HOW TO

- **overcome your fear of public speaking**
- **use energy to make your presentations more effective**
- **make eye contact with your audience**
- **develop an effective message**
- **conduct a listener analysis before you speak**
- **use visual aids**
- **create a powerful opening for your presentation**
- **organize the body of your speech**
- **apply the skills of public speaking when you give oral reports**

DEALING WITH STAGE FRIGHT

Why do so many people dread the prospect of giving a speech? Perhaps they're afraid of making a mistake or saying something foolish in front of so many people. The audience might laugh at them, or worse yet, get up and leave the room. Stage fright, as this fear is called, affects everyone. Even seasoned actors admit that they suffer from stage fright, too. As the moment arrives when you're supposed to give a presentation, a chemical called adrenalin is released inside your body. Your legs start to feel wobbly, your mouth feels dry, and your palms begin to sweat. But even though you're not aware of it, something else is happening. Adrenalin is energizing you. You become more mentally alert, your heart rate increases, your muscles get stronger. Instead of letting stage fright undermine your effectiveness as a speaker, you can actually use this adrenal energy to make your presentations more successful.

As you stand up to speak, open your arms and begin to use dynamic gestures to emphasize what you're saying. Open your mouth wide and start to speak loudly. Suddenly you'll discover that much of your stage fright will begin to disappear. The adrenal energy will be directed into your voice and your gestures.

When people have a positive response to you, 55 percent is a response to your gestures and expressions, 37 percent is a response to your voice, and 8 percent is a response to the words you say.

ENERGY IN THE G(ESTURE)-FORCE

Whenever you stand up and speak to an audience, you present a visual image. Most people are used to seeing stimulating images because they watch television and go to the movies. If the images seem uninteresting, they're apt to use their clicker and switch to another channel or they might decide to walk out of the movie theater. Listeners might do the same thing when you speak—they will mentally tune out if you present a boring visual image when you stand up in front of them. One way to make yourself more visually stimulating is to use expansive gestures and other types of body language. Here are a few things to remember.

- *Ineffective speakers present a boring image.* Some keep their hands at their sides throughout the entire presentation. Other speakers hold their hands together in front of them, or constantly wring their hands. This gives the impression that they are nervous and distracts the audience from listening to their words.
- *Effective speakers use gestures to emphasize important points.* For example, they jab a forefinger in the air to stress a word or phrase. They may also chop the air with a hand to underline the importance of a key idea. This adds emphasis to what they're saying.
- *Effective speakers use gestures to describe concepts they are presenting.* If they say "Let's increase classroom performance," they might raise an arm over their head to indicate that increase. If they say "All of us here today are in agreement," they might spread out their arms to include everyone in the room. These types of gestures add interest to what they're saying by creating a more stimulating visual image.
- *Effective speakers know that the way you stand is also important.* They don't slouch. This suggests that they're not interested in their presentation. Instead, they stand up straight with their legs slightly apart and their weight evenly distributed on both feet. This enhances their presence in front of an audience and adds authority to what they say.
- *Effective speakers know that the way they dress contributes to their visual image.* They try to dress appropriately, the way people in

their audience dress. They avoid flashy clothes and jewelry that may focus the audience's attention on what they're wearing rather than on their message.

FACIAL EXPRESSIONS

Remember, facial expressions form part of your visual image too. When you begin a talk, smile at your audience. This creates an instant connection between you and your listeners. A smile is your way of making them feel that they're part of your presentation. Another way of connecting with your listeners is through eye contact. Indeed, your eyes are one of the most valuable tools you possess as a speaker.

THE EYES HAVE IT

Here are some things to remember when you use your eyes during a presentation.

- **Don't look at the ground as you speak or over the heads of the audience. This sends a message that you're not interested in your listeners.**
- **Look at one person in the audience as you deliver a thought. Once you complete that thought, move on to another person and present your next thought. Continue this approach throughout the entire presentation.**
- **Establish eye contact with a person in the middle of the room as you begin your talk. Then select someone on one side, go back to the middle again, then move to the other side. In this way, you'll be including listeners from the entire audience.**

A smile creates an instant connection between you and your listeners.

- **<u>Establish eye contact with an individual listener to help you control your stage fright.</u> Instead of trying to talk to everyone at once, which may seem overwhelming, reduce your presentation to a one-on-one discussion with a single individual. This will be almost the same as having a conversation.**

VOCAL ENERGY

Good speakers know that there is great power in their voice. Listen to an audio recording of a speech by the Reverend Dr. Martin Luther King, Jr., and you will understand why his voice inspired millions of Americans. A good speaking voice will also help you command the attention of your listeners. Unfortunately, some speakers seem to forget this. They speak in a low monotone guaranteed to bore their listeners. Learn to vary the sound of your voice, and you will become a better speaker.

- *Raise the volume of your voice to emphasize important words and phrases.* This will show your commitment to what you're saying and help your audience remember it.
- *Use a pause when you are about to say something especially significant.* Example: "The primary cause of lung cancer is this: (pause) smoking." The pause provides a second of anticipa-

Present your information with clarity. Don't try to impress anyone with your vocabulary.

tion among your listeners. They are waiting to hear what you're going to say next, and this rivets their attention on your words even more closely.

- *Avoid the use of filler words when you speak.* These include um, uh, and you know. These words are meaningless, and they detract from the significant things you're trying to say.
- *Don't mumble.* Enunciate your words clearly so the audience can understand them. Otherwise, you risk losing your listeners' interest in your presentation.

IT'S WHAT YOU SAY AS WELL AS HOW YOU SAY IT

An excellent way to improve your presentation skills is to observe the way that other speakers deliver their talks. The next time you attend a school assembly or a student council meeting, evaluate the way the speaker uses gestures to underscore his main points. How well does he make eye contact with his listeners? Does he change the volume of his voice to emphasize key words and phrases? As you already know, all these elements contribute to the effectiveness of a presentation.

Of course, your delivery is only one facet of a good talk. What you say is important, too. A successful presentation must contain *substance:* Your ideas should not be tired cliches that the audience has heard before. Make sure the information is new to your listeners so they will pay attention. A good talk should *appeal* to your listeners. If you bore them with a dry recitation of facts, they will lose interest. Dress up the data with examples and anecdotes to illustrate your points. *Structure* the material and organize the ideas logically so they make sense to your audience. Otherwise, your talk may be too difficult to follow. Finally, present the information with *clarity.* All the words you use should be simple and easy to understand. Don't try to impress anyone with your vocabulary.

Each day 80,000 people in the United States speak to audiences.

WHAT'S YOUR PURPOSE?

As you begin to figure out what you're going to say in a presentation, ask yourself this question: What's the purpose of my talk? Like a written report, speeches can have several different purposes. Some simply **present information.** For example, you might be talking to your science class on the weather phenomenon known as El Niño. Your presentation might point out why scientists believe El Niño occurs and the impact it has on the weather in the United States. Some talks are primarily designed to **explain a process.** Suppose you worked at an animal shelter. Your supervisor might ask you to speak to new employees and explain the procedure for checking in stray animals. Sometimes the primary purpose of a talk is to **persuade.** You might be giving a talk to the student body trying to persuade students to vote for you because you would make the best student body president. Persuasive talks often end with a call for action—that is, you want your listeners to do something. In this case, you might ask them at the end of the talk to vote for you.

Frequently, talks serve more than one purpose. For example, you might present information on homelessness in your community. This is designed to convince your listeners to become aware that there is a need for volunteers in homeless shelters. Finally, you might ask them to sign up for volunteer work at a nearby shelter that is run by one of the local churches.

DELIVERING A MESSAGE

The most important single piece of information you deliver in a presentation is your message. The message should not be confused with the topic. It's what you want to say about the topic—your main point. This is similar to the theme in a written report. For example, your topic might be the school baseball team. Your message could be that baseball practice should begin two weeks earlier so the team would be better prepared for its season. Here are some key points to remember about your message:

- *Deliver the message early, usually in the opening of your presentation.* This way the audience will know right away what point you're trying to make in your talk. As a listener, there's nothing worse than trying to figure out the main idea the speaker wants to deliver. Your audience can easily tune out.
- *Make sure that all the information in your talk relates to the main message.* Anything that doesn't should be eliminated. Most audiences do not enjoy long-winded talks with a lot of superfluous information. Listeners want you to get to the point right away and stay on the point all the way through your presentation.
- *Deliver the message more than once.* It would be wonderful to imagine that you have to mention your main point only one time and the audience will remember it. But your listeners are not as familiar with the message as you are, and they need to be reminded from time to time what it is. Introduce the mes-

sage at the beginning of your talk. Then mention it again in the body of your speech. Finally, restate the message at the conclusion of your presentation.

- *Remember KISS. Keep it simple, students.* The message should be as simple as possible. Indeed, you should be able to state it in a sentence. If you can't, it may be because you aren't quite sure what the message is.
- *Start with the message.* Before you do any other work on a presentation, define the message. This will serve as your guiding principle as you prepare the talk. The message will enable you to determine what to put in the opening of your speech, which points to include in the body of your presentation, and how to shape your conclusion.

Abraham Lincoln's Gettysburg Address, the most famous speech ever delivered by a president of the United States, was only 268 words long.

CONDUCT A LISTENER ANALYSIS

The reason you give a speech is to communicate with your listeners. No communication is complete unless the audience receives your message and understands your ideas. After you've defined your message, begin to think about the listeners. Here are questions to ask yourself to help prepare an effective speach.

1. *What do they know?* You must always be aware of your listeners' level of understanding. Don't start to use words that are over their heads. Complicated computer terminology, for example, won't make any sense to an audience that doesn't know very much about computers. Listeners will simply lose

interest in what you're trying to tell them. On the other hand, there's no need to waste time explaining terms that your audience already understands. This just sounds condescending. And there's no quicker way to turn off your listeners than for them to feel that you think you're smarter than they are.

2. *What is their attitude?* If you're trying to persuade your listeners to adopt your point of view, it helps to know whether they're inclined to be on your side or whether they're inclined to side against you. Suppose you're talking to the board of education about expanding the music program in your school. If most members are opposed, you'll have to use a lot of convincing arguments to change their minds.

3. *What appeals to them?* If you're trying to convince members of the board to enlarge the music program, it will help to know what types of arguments will appeal to them. If they're worried about money, for example, you better be able to show that an expanded program won't cost very much. Otherwise, your presentation won't be very successful. Put yourself in the listeners' place. Try to figure out what they're concerned about and what is likely to interest them.

"When I get ready to talk to people, I spend two-thirds of the time thinking about what they want to hear and one-third thinking about what I want to say."

—Abraham Lincoln

VISUAL AIDS

Speakers often rely on visual aids as a method of presenting information to their audience. Experts believe that people are more likely to remember ideas when they see them as well as hear them.

People are more likely to remember ideas that they see as well as hear.

A few words on a flip chart or poster board can reinforce an important idea from your talk. Instead of using hundreds of words, you can present a single chart or graph. This will often depict the information you're trying to present far more easily.

One of the simplest types of visual aids is a list of key points. You might put this up at the beginning of your talk and refer to it as you make your presentation. In this way, listeners will be constantly reminded of the main ideas that you'll be covering. Suppose you're talking at a school assembly, trying to persuade students to volunteer their time to plant trees in the community. In support of your position, you are presenting three central arguments. List these on a poster board so the audience will not forget them.

WHY WE SHOULD PLANT TREES

1. **beautify the community**
2. **reduce pollution and erosion**
3. **provide food and homes for animals**

Keep your visual aid as simple as possible. At the top, use a headline that underscores the message of your presentation. Make sure you list only a few points and state them as simply as possible. If you use too many words, the visual aid can easily appear cluttered, and your audience will find it hard to read.

Other common types of visual aids are graphs and charts. You've seen them in math class. Bar graphs, for example, compare several items. Suppose four schools with different size student populations are going to participate in the tree planting project. You can use a bar graph to compare the number of trees each school will be responsible for planting. Pie charts break something up into its parts. These parts must add up to 100 percent. For instance, you might want to plant five different species of trees. On a pie chart, you can show what percentage of all the trees each species represents.

Visual aids are an effective way to keep your audience involved in your presentation. You need only one or two during a talk. But they can help you make sure your ideas will not be forgotten.

MEMORY TRICK:

I E R

One of the best ways to ensure that audiences will remember what you say is to use an approach called IER.

INTRODUCE your message in the beginning of the presentation.
EXPLAIN the message in the body of your talk by presenting all the ideas to back it up. This should include several key points as well as the evidence to support them. The evidence might consist of statistics, examples, and other types of data.

REPEAT the message. If you're delivering a persuasive presentation, you might also add a call to action at the end of the presentation, so your audience will know what to do after listening to your speech.

AT THE PODIUM

THUMBS UP

Use gestures to emphasize main points and describe the concepts you're presenting.

Vary the sound of your voice, raising and lowering the volume.

Establish eye contact with your listeners so you can connect with them.

Give your talk plenty of substance and structure it so listeners will be able to follow the flow of your ideas.

Make the message clear and deliver it early in the talk. Then repeat it in the body and at the conclusion.

THUMBS DOWN

Speak with your hands constantly at your sides.

Talk in a dull monotone, never varying the volume and use filler words, such as "um", and "you know".

Look at the floor while you speak, suggesting eye contact is not important.

Don't worry about the substance or structure of the talk, just focus on the delivery.

Keep the message vague—and wait until the end to deliver it.

SUPER TACTIC

USE SOLID SOURCES

From time to time, everyone has to stand up and deliver an oral report in school. Perhaps you're asked to make a report to the class in English or social studies. Or you may be a member of a club or

other extracurricular group and have to present a report at a meeting. Suppose you are a member of the student council, and at the next meeting you are going to present a proposal to hold a career day so students can find out about part-time jobs and volunteer opportunities available during summer vacation. A good report must be based on more than the speaker's opinion. It requires sound, practical ideas, supported by hard evidence—statistics, examples, and other types of information. You can rely on several types of sources to provide evidence for your report.

- Books and Articles. One source of data is printed material that can usually be found in the library. For example, look for magazine articles about similar types of career days held in other schools. In some cases, hard copies of the magazines are stored in the library. Full-text versions of some articles are available on-line from the library's computer, and you can make printouts to use in preparing your presentation.
- Interviews. Call local businesses and volunteer organizations to find out if they would be willing to participate in a career day. Interview teachers at another school that conducted a similar program and use quotes from these interviews in your report. In addition, the Internet provides an opportunity to exchange information about important topics. A conversation in cyberspace can provide a valuable source of quotes and anecdotes.
- Surveys. Through a simple survey, or questionnaire, you can find out how many other students are in favor of a career day. The questionnaire can also ask students for suggestions that would help make the event successful.

These three sources of data give you all the evidence you need to put together a presentation.

FINDING AN OPENING

If you don't hook your audience in the first few minutes, they may tune you out. Remember, they're used to watching media and they want to be stimulated immediately. They don't want to wait. That's the reason the opening of your presentation is the most critical part. Indeed, you can make or break a talk right there. It's not enough simply to present the message. You also need a hook—a way of presenting that opening that will make the listeners sit up and pay attention. Usually, you can find the hook in the data you've collected. Here are some hooks that provide attention-grabbing openings.

- A startling statistic. Begin with a fact or statistic that the audience is not likely to know and that is sure to surprise them. For example, you may have discovered that 80 percent of the student body, based on the results of your questionnaire, support a school career day. That's the type of statistic that is likely to impress an audience that your proposal is a good one.
- An incident from the media. Sometimes a story appears in the newspapers or on television that is directly related to your message. Because of its immediacy, the story can provide a very effective opening for your presentation.
- A quotation. Perhaps you discovered a good quote from your interviews or your research in the library. You could open your talk with this quote, as long as it supports your message.
- The personal story. Tell a story from your own experience. This personalizes your presentation and creates an instant bond between you and your listeners. You might point out that you could have found a much better job last summer if the school had held a career day.
- A famous example. Use an example about someone who is well

known to introduce your message. In your research, you may have discovered a famous person who discovered his or her lifework through a summer job.

KEEPING IDEAS IN ORDER

Good speakers know that ideas must be presented in a clear, logical order to ensure that listeners understand them. A presentation should begin with the hook and the message. Then it should flow along smoothly through a series of key points that support that message. These ideas form the body of the speech. In a talk, there are several ways of organizing the points so listeners can follow them easily.

- Chronological order. If you're presenting a report on a famous person, you might discuss her life chronologically—beginning with her childhood and continuing until her death. Speakers also use chronology when they explain the steps in a process. "First, you do this; second, you do this; third, you do this...."
- Problem...Solution. This is another simple approach to presenting information. A speaker begins by explaining the problem. Example: "Students are unaware of job opportunities in the community." Then the speaker presents a solution: a schoolwide career day to be held in early May. The solution is supported by data from other schools that have held career days. Finally, the speaker explains how the project will be carried out.
- Most important...least important. You've probably heard this type of presentation. The speaker begins with a message, then presents three details to support it. First, he states the most important detail, backing it up with evidence. This is followed by a second detail, then a final one. Many experts believe that a speaker should save the least important detail until last. By

hitting the audience with the most convincing detail at the beginning, it immediately wins them over to the speaker's side.

- Combination. Many talks use a combination of structures to present information. For example, you might begin your report by describing the problem. Then you might present three details to support your solution—a career day. Finally, you might describe a step-by-step process to make the career day a reality.

PREPARATION AND PRACTICE

Very few speakers have the ability to give a good talk right off the top of their heads. It takes preparation and practice. There are seven key steps that you should always follow in preparing an oral report.

1. Define your message.
2. Present only the ideas that relate to your message.
3. Conduct an audience analysis.
4. Support your ideas with hard evidence.
5. Create an effective opening.
6. Present your ideas in a logical order within the body of your presentation.
7. Restate your message at the conclusion of your presentation.

Once you finish preparing a presentation, take some time to practice your delivery. This will enable you to make a good impression on the audience when you actually stand up and give the oral report. Some speakers try to memorize their entire presentation. But this is a very risky approach. If you become nervous due to stage fright, you're apt to forget an important point, which will throw off the entire flow of your report. As a result, you may not be able to remember the rest of your presentation. This can be extremely embarrassing.

Other speakers decide to read their entire report. They feel very comfortable having the speech in front of them. These speakers usually place their report on a lectern—a high table with a slanted top that holds the written speech. Then they read their report from beginning to end, barely looking at their audience during the presentation.

There are several problems with this approach. First, it prevents the speakers from looking at their audience and making eye contact with their listeners. Second, speakers often hold on to the lectern while they're speaking. As a result, they never use any gestures during their speech. This reduces the amount of energy that goes into the presentation. Third, the speakers may be so intent on delivering every word in the prepared text that they forget to put any enthusiasm in their voice. Instead, the speech is delivered in a boring monotone. Remember, more than 90 percent of an audiences's response is to the speaker's voice and gestures. Only 8 percent is to the speaker's words. Without energy, the talk will fall completely flat.

The best method of delivering a report is to use a few note cards. Write down your key ideas on the cards, and refer to them whenever you need to remind yourself of what to say. In this way, you can speak directly to the audience without breaking eye contact during most of your presentation. You can also focus on using gestures and your voice to add emphasis to important ideas.

Don't forget to practice your gestures and vocal energy as you prepare for a presentation. Stand in front of a mirror and observe yourself as you speak. You might also tape record your presentation and play it back to listen to your voice. If it needs more volume, deliver the talk again and try to raise the level of your voice.

Another effective way to practice is to ask a friend or member of your family to listen to your presentation and give you feedback. This will enable you to make improvements.

THE Q & A SESSION

At the end of a presentation, some people in the audience may want to ask questions. As a speaker, you can prepare for this Q & A session, just the way the president of the United States does before he holds a press conference. The president anticipates most of the questions that reporters are likely to ask him. He prepares his answers in advance and practices them before appearing in front of the television cameras. You can do the same thing as you get ready to give your talk.

1. Think about the type of questions that are likely to be asked by the audience. For example, suppose you realize that someone might want to know how much time students would need to commit to the career day to make it successful. Think about this issue and prepare your answer.
2. Practice for the Q & A session. Have a friend or family member ask you questions and practice handling them.
3. Don't fake it if you don't know. Sometimes you may not have the information at your fingertips to answer a question. Don't pretend you know the answer, if you don't. You might easily make a mistake, and someone in the audience might catch it. This will undermine your credibility. Tell the person who asked the question that you'll get the information and give it to her later.
4. Listen until the person has finished asking the question. Some speakers interrupt and start answering before the question is completed. This is rude; and the speaker may misinterpret the question and answer it incorrectly.
5. Repeat the question aloud before you answer it. If you're speaking in front of a large group, some people may not have heard the question. Therefore, your answer will make no sense to them unless you repeat the question before answering it.
6. Look at the person asking the question as you answer it. This is another occasion when eye contact is important.

Public speaking is a skill that almost anyone can learn. Students who are powerful speakers stand out because they know how to present ideas successfully. These same people often become leaders of large companies and civic groups because they know how to persuade others to follow them. You can be one of these leaders too, if you practice the elements of successful public speaking.

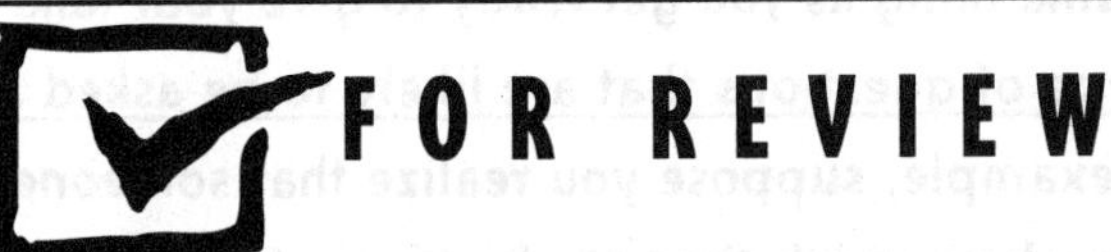

FOR REVIEW

1. How can you overcome stage fright?
2. How can you use gestures to make a presentation more interesting?
3. Why is eye contact with your listeners so important?
4. What are the elements of vocal energy?
5. What makes a successful message?
6. How do you conduct a listener analysis?
7. How can visual aids make a speech more effective?
8. What are several types of powerful openings for oral reports?
9. How can you organize information in the body of an oral report?
10. What should you do to practice a report before delivering a presentation?

10 TIME MANAGEMENT

Have you ever had one of those days when there seemed to be too much to do and not enough time to get all of it accomplished? It's easy to feel that way in school. There are always classes to attend, tests to study for, and papers to write. On top of that, there are extracurricular activities, such as sports, the school newspaper, the debating team, and band. Some students also hold down part-time jobs. Getting everything done, doing things well, and finishing them on time can be a real challenge. Time management can help you handle all your responsibilities by utilizing the hours in each day to maximum efficiency.

Some people fear time management means intensive planning and rigid schedules with no opportunity for fun and relaxation. They're wrong. All that's required is learning and using a few simple techniques that will enable you to accomplish more in less time so you'll become more successful.

IN THIS CHAPTER, YOU'LL LEARN HOW TO

- **overcome procrastination**
- **deal with distractions that may be causing you to waste a lot of time**
- **organize your workspace more efficiently**
- **create an activities' list for the week**
- **prioritize activities so you'll always do first things first**

- **develop a realistic schedule**
- **apply time management skills to accomplish long-term projects**

DO YOU PROCRASTINATE?

"Most of us procrastinate in one area or another," explain Ronni Eisenberg and Kate Kelly in their book *Organize Yourself!* "Some people procrastinate about everything." You probably have projects you don't like to do—like cleaning up a messy closet or studying a least favorite subject—so you tend to put them off and get around to them only after you've finished other things. That's a mild form of procrastination. On the other hand, you may be one of those people for whom procrastination has almost become a way of life. Whatever the project, you seem unable to get down to starting it until the last minute. Unfortunately, putting it off does not make it go away. No matter how long you wait, that term paper is still there, and the due date hasn't changed. Instead, as the date gets closer, you probably find yourself worrying more and more about it. Then, as you rush to finish on time, your stress level gets higher and higher. Perhaps you stay up late the night before the paper's due, feverishly finishing it on the computer. The next day, you're exhausted—you hand in the paper on time but don't really feel very good about it. "If I'd only started sooner," you say to yourself, "I could have done a much better job."

Why didn't you start sooner? Experts tell us that people tend to procrastinate for a variety of reasons.

- *"I just can't face it."* Some tasks seem so formidable that you just can't bring yourself to begin them. You look at everything that's involved—all the steps and how long each one is likely to take—and you start to groan. It's much easier to put the whole thing out of your mind and forget about it entirely.

- *"Why worry? It's so far away."* Some projects have a long timeline. It's several weeks before they'll be due—plenty of time to worry about them later. Unfortunately, "later" seems to arrive very quickly. The date is here before you know it, and you're forced to hurry up and finish everything at the last minute.
- *"It might not be perfect."* Are you a perfectionist? No matter what the task, do you have to do it exactly right? You go over each English paper again and again, looking for every misplaced comma. You check, double check, and triple check your math homework to make sure there are no mistakes anywhere. Perfectionism is admirable—up to a point. But it can get in the way of starting new projects. Trying to be perfect can be a terrible burden, making every task seem so overwhelming that it can make you hesitate to start.
- *"It won't take much time anyway."* Sometimes you don't get started on a task soon enough because you underestimate how much time it will take to complete. That science assignment, for example, may seem easy. So you leave it until the study hall just before class, figuring an hour will be plenty of time to complete it. After getting started, however, you find out it's going to take much longer than you thought. As a result of procrastinating, you're going to be late handing in the assignment.
- *"I don't like it."* Probably the most common reason for putting off a school assignment is also the simplest. You simply don't enjoy the work, whatever it is, and you'd rather be having fun doing something else. After all, it's probably much more fun to watch your favorite television show or talk to your friends on the telephone than to complete your Spanish homework. So you put it off...and put it off...and put it off...and perhaps it never gets done.

Time management experts believe most of us need to increase the amount of time we budget to complete a task by approximately 25 percent.

SUPER STRATEGY

PUT PROCRASTINATION BEHIND YOU

You probably spend as much energy procrastinating and worrying about doing a task as actually doing it. The only difference is that the work is actually done and you don't have to think about it any longer. What's more, you have the satisfaction of knowing that it's been completed. So why not stop procrastinating and actually get down to work? Here are some tips that may help.

- Do what you don't like, then what you like. If you can't seem to force yourself to sit down in front of your homework, try to look beyond the dry assignment to something more pleasurable. Make a deal with yourself to spend an hour working, then take a break. Call a friend on the telephone, have a snack, surf the Internet. Break up your homework schedule this way: work...free time...work...free time, etc. Then fill the free time with things you like to do. You'll find it's far easier to get down to work.
- Remember, big projects are made up of little ones. If a long assignment seems overwhelming to you, it may be because you're trying to focus on too much at once. You don't swallow an entire meal in one gulp, you break it down into bite-sized pieces. It's the same way with large projects. A term paper, for instance, involves research, outlining, writing, and revising. It's easy to

feel frustrated if you think about all these tasks at once. Instead, just start with the first step—the research—and take it one book at a time. You'll be surprised how much more pleasurable it will be if you approach it this way. If you regard the large project as a series of small ones, they'll seem far more manageable.

- Cut yourself some slack. Perfection isn't something that human beings attain, and you're not likely to be an exception. No project has to be done perfectly. The best you can give it is just that—your best. So dive in and assume you'll probably make some mistakes. That's the way most people learn how to do things. Anyway, you don't need an A+ on every assignment. What's more, you can enjoy the process of doing a project far more if you aren't constantly second-guessing yourself.
- Leave yourself time. When everything is left until the last minute, there's very little you can do when something takes longer than you thought it would. Don't let that happen to you. Start an assignment earlier rather than later and give yourself some extra time. Even if you've done similar types of geometry problems before and you thought they took only 45 minutes, your memory might not be as accurate as you think. Most people tend to underestimate the amount of time it takes to do things. And this is even more likely to occur with a task you haven't done before.
- Set some goals for yourself. If you want to reduce procrastination, don't try to do it all at once. Establish some realistic goals and strive to achieve them. Try starting your homework 30 minutes earlier each day for a week to see how much difference it makes in what you can accomplish. Monitor your progress at the end of the week. Did you get enough work done? If you're still not allowing enough time to finish everything, add another 30 minutes to your homework schedule and repeat the same process. Use a similar approach with long-term assignments. Start the project

a few days earlier than you'd usually begin a project. If this still doesn't give you enough time to complete it satisfactorily, add more time when you do the next project.

DEALING WITH DISTRACTIONS

One reason it's so difficult to conquer procrastination is that so many distractions seem to stand between you and your work. Imagine if you lived a century ago. There would have been no television or radio, no Internet or CD players to distract you. Indeed, the telephone was still a relatively new invention, and very few people had one in their homes. Now you have all these distractions to interrupt your work—if you let them. You have a choice: They can control you, or you can control them. Don't procrastinate! The time to start removing distractions is now.

Telephone calls. Perhaps the most intrusive sound in anyone's life is the insistent ring of the telephone. It may also be the hardest to resist. No matter what you're doing, it's so tempting to pick up the phone and find out who's on the other end. Maybe it's someone inviting you to a party, or someone bursting to tell you the latest gossip about a friend at school. If you don't answer the phone, you tell yourself, you might never receive that important message. But if you're in the midst of studying, a telephone call can easily become a distraction that pulls you away from your work. And the longer you stay on the phone, the harder it will be to return to working.

How do you deal with telephone interruptions? One way is to limit the length of the calls. Some conversations are easy. The caller wants to give you some brief information that will take only a couple of minutes; then you can go back to work. But what if the call is going to last longer? How should you handle it? You might say, "I'm sorry. I'd really like to talk further, but I'm study-

If you are in the midst of studying, a telephone call can easily become a distraction that pulls you away from your work.

ing right now. Would you mind if I called you back later when I take a break?" This enables you to take the call, stay on long enough to find out why the caller has phoned you, and if it's going to be a long conversation, delay it until later.

Another approach is to screen your calls by using an answering machine. Instead of interrupting your homework, you let the machine handle everything. Then you can check your messages when you're taking a break or after you've completely finished your homework and return any calls that seem important. This enables you to control the telephone.

The media. How much time do you spend watching television, listening to music on the radio or CD player, or surfing the Internet? It may be far more than you think. Keep track of all your "media hours" for a week and write them down in a notebook. You may be surprised at how much of your time is being devoted to these activities—time that might be better spent on school work. This doesn't mean you can't study with background music from the radio or CD player. But music can easily become a distraction preventing you from finishing assignments on time.

What can you do about it? Don't try to stop watching television entirely. Instead, start whittling away, little by little, at the number of your media hours. Cut 30 minutes off this week; one hour, next; one and one-half hours, the week after. Fill that time with additional studying. Then chart its effect on your grades. Have they improved at the end of a marking period? Are they still not as high as you'd like them to be? If so, perhaps you should reduce the number of your media hours even further.

Snacking, snoozing, and staring out the window. People have various patterns of working. Some seem to do best when they sit for long periods of time—two hours or more—intensely doing a project. Others seems to work better in smaller chunks—one-hour or 45-minute segments. Then there are others who are bounding up from their desks every few minutes to check their e-mail or go to the refrigerator for a snack. They come back to their desks, start to work again, only to begin staring out the window and daydreaming. A short time later, they heave a big sigh or yawn loudly and, before they know it, they're lying down on the bed taking a rest. It's impossible to get any real work accomplished when you leave your desk regularly to do something other than study. A snack or a nap is fine, but you should use them as rewards for getting some work done.

Precious minutes. Time management means learning to use all blocks of time efficiently—no matter how large or how small they may be. If you're planning to do research at the library, a two-hour chunk of time on Saturday may be necessary to make some significant headway with the reference materials. Likewise, an after-school job may also require you to set aside a sizeable block of time several days each week. But for other projects, small bites of time may be extremely valuable. It's easy to overlook such opportunities and squander these precious moments doing nothing. Suppose you find yourself with a few extra minutes before lunch, you might be able to use this time effectively to learn some vocabulary words for your Spanish classs. Or you may be sitting in the school auditorium waiting for your play rehearsal to begin. This short time segment may be all you need to review your science notes for a class discussion during first period the following morning. Of course, you don't need to fill every moment of the day with some kind of work. But so-called down time can often prove extremely valuable in getting tasks accomplished.

ORGANIZING YOUR WORKSPACE

It's difficult to study efficiently if you have a disorganized, uncomfortable work area. Most people find they work best in a room that is fairly neat and organized. Here are a few guidelines that may help you improve the place where you currently work.

- *A little neatness makes a big difference.* Some students work in the midst of chaos. Their rooms are strewn with books and papers, clothing, and empty food wrappers. If you ask them, these students claim that it is easy for them to find everything they need in that awful mess. But the truth is, that in order to do their homework, they often waste valuable time looking for important notes and research materials. You can save at least one-half hour a day by keeping your workspace neat.
- *A simple organizing system really helps.* It doesn't take very much to organize all the resources you need to work efficiently. For class notes, it's probably a good idea to buy yourself a notebook with separators for each subject. This prevents confusion and gives you plenty of paper for taking notes. Another invaluable organizing tool is a file folder. Instead of stuffing those old quizzes and compositions into your textbooks until the binding breaks, label a folder for each course and use it to store your papers. These folders may prove extremely valuable when it comes time to study for final exams. You can also create a file folder for a term paper or

other long project. If you keep the folders stored in a file organizer on your desk, they won't be hard to find when you need them. At the end of the semester, put all the folders in a file cabinet. They're out of the way and not taking up valuable space on your desk, but they're still available if you want to refer to them in the future.

- *An efficient workspace is important.* Every efficient workspace needs three basic components: a comfortable chair, a desk or other wide, flat surface on which to write; and good lighting. You might also consider purchasing a simple plastic organizer, or desk caddy, for storing your pens and pencils, rulers, and paper clips. Finally, a small inexpensive clock is helpful so you can keep yourself on schedule as you work.

"Having a clean desk and a more organized schedule is helping me to do more and feel better right here and now."
—Gwenda Blair, Writer

DEVELOPING YOUR SCHEDULE: STEP BY STEP

As you begin to organize your study space, reduce your time wasters, and rid yourself of procrastination, you can also start developing a realistic weekly work schedule. This is a schedule that will enable you to focus on the most important tasks in your life, deal with emergency situations as they come along, and still leave you with plenty of time to have fun. Developing this schedule involves a simple three-step process.

STEP ONE: FIGURE OUT YOUR ACTIVITIES LIST

A schedule is comprised of activities—classes to attend, papers to write, household chores to do, etc. The way to begin preparing a schedule is to make a list at the beginning of the week of all the activities you have to accomplish each day. On weekdays, of course, you'll always have classes to attend and homework to do. But there may be other activities as well. On Wednesday and Thursday, for example, your list might include the following:

WEDNESDAY	THURSDAY
start Spanish project	study for science test on Friday
take driving lesson	plan article for yearbook
shop at mall with friends	write first draft of book report
	for history
study for math test Thursday	play basketball with friends
	after school
attend debate club meeting	call about job interview at
	supermarket
go swimming at Y	pick up contact lenses

It's a good idea to keep your activities list in a small notebook you can carry in your pocket or backpack. Keep the notebook with you at all times, and write down new activities for your list as they occur. Suppose you're sitting in English class and your teacher suddenly announces a special homework assignment due the following day. That information belongs on your list. Don't trust your memory. If the president of the nature club tells you that a special meeting is being called for 2:30 on Friday, make a note of it on your activities list. This list is an extremely valuable tool in helping you keep track of short-term as well as long-term projects. Once you get in the habit of maintaining a list in junior high or high school, you can use the same technique after you start college where there may be far more work to handle. Busy managers in large organizations also find this type of list essential, since they have many meetings to attend and projects to juggle in their demanding jobs.

STEP TWO: PRIORITIZE YOUR LIST OF ACTIVITIES

Some days just don't seem to contain enough hours for you to do everything on your activities list and still have time left for classes and regular homework assignments. Therefore, you must set some priorities for yourself. Go back to your list of activities for Wednesday and Thursday. Certainly, studying for your math and science tests are a high priority. You may also need to write the first draft of the book report, because the final paper is due on Monday. Your parents have been after you to start driving lessons and pick up your contact lenses, so you'd better get those jobs done too. And you love debating, so you don't want to miss the meeting. These are your *top* priorities. So label them T on your activities' list. The article for the yearbook, the job interview, swimming at the Y, and starting the Spanish project are also important. These are *medium* priorities—things you'd really like to accomplish. Label them M. The *lowest* priorities are shopping at the mall and playing basketball—you'll do them if you have time. Label them L.

WEDNESDAY	THURSDAY
M start Spanish project	T study for science test on Friday
T take driving lesson	M plan article for yearbook
L shop at mall with friends	T write first draft of book report for history
T study for math test Thursday	L play basketball with friends after school
T attend debate club meeting	M call about job interview at supermarket
M go swimming at Y	T pick up contact lenses

When you put together your list, all these priorities make sense. Wednesday runs smoothly—you get all of the important activities accomplished. Then the unexpected happens. On Thursday, your English teacher announces a special homework assignment due the next day. Suddenly this becomes a top priority. Instead of writing the first draft of the yearbook article, you'll have to devote that time to reviewing your history notes. If you have time left afterward, you can work on your article. Or you might have to postpone it until the following week and make it a top priority. By prioritizing your activities, you always ensure there's enough time to get the most important things accomplished. Low priority activities can be done if you have time left over.

STEP THREE: CREATE A WEEKLY SCHEDULE

Once you've made a list of activities and prioritized them, you're ready to transfer all this information to a weekly schedule. No schedule is cast in stone. It's always subject to change as new activities arise and priorities shift. But the schedule helps you organize each week effectively. Although it takes a little extra time to put together a schedule at the beginning of each week, the benefits are substantial.

- You're far less likely to forget an important appointment.
- The schedule will help you avoid the embarassment of being late. People who are constantly late earn a reputation for being unreliable and undisciplined. What's more, turning in projects late can often cost you points in your grades.
- You achieve more control of your life. The schedule enables you to plan ahead. If an unexpected quiz arises for Friday, you can look at your schedule and figure out what other activity to move and where to move it so it will still be finished on time.
- The schedule helps you avoid the problem of making two separate appointments for the same time.

As you put together your schedule, make sure to leave time for traveling from one place to another. And don't forget to use those small blocks of time discussed earlier. Your schedule should be as realistic as possible. Build in time for snacks, telephone calls, and even a television break to watch your favorite program. Here's the schedule for Thursday, integrating the items from the activities list.

THURSDAY

8:00-8:30	travel to school
8:30-9:30	science class
9:30-10:30	study hall (review history notes for class discussion)
10:30-11:30	history class
11:30-12:15	lunch (review Spanish vocabulary for class)
12:15-1:55	English class
1:55-2:15	Spanish class
2:15-2:30	homeroom
2:45-3:30	pick up contact lenses
3:30-4:00	travel home
4:00-4:30	call supermarket about job
4:30-6:00	Do English homework
6:00-7:00	dinner
7:00-8:00	study for science test
8:00-9:00	tv
9:00-11:00	write book report

WHEN DO YOU STUDY BEST?

Making a study schedule may take some trial and error. Everyone has different times of the day when he or she studies best. For example, you may be a morning person and do your best work from 5AM to 7AM. Therefore, writing a book report from 9PM to 11PM may turn out to be the worst time for you to do this kind of work. You're tired by that hour and can't think too clearly. You'd be much better off getting up early in the morning. It's important to schedule difficult work for the time of day when you're the sharpest. Save something that's much easier for the hours just before you go to bed.

GETTING THINGS DONE

THUMBS UP

Don't procrastinate. It's better to get your work done now than to put it off until later when you might run out of time.

Control distractions, such as telephone calls and watching television. They can cause you to lose concentration.

Learn to use small blocks of time wisely. This will give you more free time.

Organize your workspace—a little neatness can save you precious time every day.

Develop a schedule. It can help you focus on the important tasks and get them done on time.

THUMBS DOWN

Live for today. There's plenty of time to do the unpleasant tasks tomorrow. By then, if you're lucky, they might go away.

Don't worry if you become distracted, you can go back to work later.

Waste time. Small blocks of time were designed for taking breaks—use them that way.

If you're comfortable working in chaos, there's no reason to make changes.

Don't develop a schedule. Schedules are too rigid. They don't give you an opportunity to do things that arise unexpectedly.

SUPER TACTICS

USING TIME MANAGEMENT FOR LONG-TERM PROJECTS

You can use the time management skills just described not only in planning your weekly assignments but also for much longer projects. The difference is that these projects are usually more complex. They consist of several different components that generally must be done in a specific order. That is, the first step must be completed—or almost completed—before you can start the next one. This requires more careful planning over a more extended timeline. Along the way, you'll need milestones to make sure that each step is being done on time and that the next step is started on schedule so that the entire project will be finished by the deadline.

Several students decided to work together on a project for their social studies class. They planned to develop a video presentation featuring two outstanding women leaders from their town to be shown during Women's History Month. They had nine weeks in which to do the video production. That may sound like ample time, but actually every part of the presentation had to be carefully planned so it would be completed by the assigned deadline.

Video presentations generally consist of three parts: preproduction, production, and postproduction. Preproduction includes all the preparation that must occur before the actual videotaping can begin: interviewing the two women; writing the script for the presentation; and deciding what pictures would need to be shot to illustrate the words. As this part neared completion, the students began the production stage. This involved scheduling times to videotape the women at work and at home; arranging to borrow the video equipment from the school's media center, and actually shooting the scenes. Postproduction included editing the scenes together in a videotape, recording a student narrator's voice to present the words, and adding music as well as special effects.

The students worked backward from the due date, figuring out when each stage would have to begin so they could finish on schedule. They tried to be as generous as possible when it came to allotting time for each task. For instance, they wanted to start early placing calls to several women. Their two top choices might not be available, so they had to have backups. The students needed to develop questions and finally to hold the interviews. They also had to scout office locations after the interviews to determine places to videotape the women doing their work, holding meetings, or talking with clients. These shots would be necessary to illustrate the script. Some of the interview material might be usable as part of the script and the soundtrack for the videotape, so the students had to check with the media center to ensure that sound equipment was available. One interview might not be enough, so the students had to leave time to schedule a second interview.

Script writing can be time-consuming. The students realized they might need several drafts before the words and the pictures worked together smoothly. Then they had to arrange shooting dates that would fit in with the availability of equipment from the media center, the women's busy schedule, as well as the students' busy schedules. If one of the women was unexpectedly sick or out of town, it would throw off the production, and the shooting would have to be rescheduled. So the students tried to build in a little extra time for emergencies. Finally, they left a couple of weeks at the end for postproduction. Since editing facilities were not available at the school's media center, they would have to arrange to do the editing at a local cable television station.

Here's the schedule the students created:

VIDEO PROJECT		
PREPRODUCTION		**Estimated Time**
Week 1		
call women leaders and arrange interviews; check with media center to make sure sound equipment is available		2 hrs.
Week 2		
conduct interviews with women scout office locations where women work for shooting		4 hrs. (includes travel)
Week 3		
transcribe interviews and begin script writing check with women to determine availability for shooting check with media center on availability of video equipment		8 hrs.
Week 4		
complete first draft of script and begin revisions reserve time at local television station for editing schedule taping dates with two women leaders		6 hrs.
Week 5		
finish script revisions storyboard script (block out shots to illustrate words)		8 hrs.
PRODUCTION		
Week 6	videotape both women in their offices	6 hrs.
Week 7	videotape both women with their families	3 hrs.
Week 8	videotape both women in community activities	3 hrs.
POSTPRODUCTION		
Week 9	edit videotape at cable television station record narration; add music and special effects	8 hrs.

MEMORY TRICK: CESD

Time management provides a structure for using all the other skills presented in this book. No matter how adept you may be at doing research and writing, notetaking and preparing for tests, you need enough time to carry out these tasks effectively.

CONQUER procrastination.
ELIMINATE time wasters.
SET priorities.
DEVELOP a realistic schedule.

Together, these things will help you create the time you need. All it takes is a little planning and a commitment to reaching the highest level of excellence that you're capable of achieving in school.

FOR REVIEW

1. Why do people procrastinate?
2. How can you overcome procrastination?
3. How can you deal with distractions that prevent you from doing your work?
4. What skills can you use to organize your workspace more effectively?
5. What is an activities list?
6. Why is it important to prioritize your activities each week?
7. How can a weekly schedule benefit you?
8. Why should you try to determine your peak hours of efficiency?
9. How do you apply time management to long-term projects?

INDEX

Q

R

S

T

U

V

W

Y